Churches

Churches

Timothy Brittain-Catlin

Collins

For Oliver

First published in 2008 by Collins,
an imprint of HarperCollins Publishers
77-85 Fulham Palace Road
Hammersmith
London W6 8JB

www.collins.co.uk

Collins is a registered trademark of HarperCollins Publishers Ltd

1 3 5 7 9 10 9 6 4 2

Text © Timothy Brittain-Catlin 2008

Editorial, picture research, design and proofreading: Basement Press, London
www.basementpress.com

A catalogue record for this book is available from the British Library

ISBN-13: 978-0-00-726306-6

Printed and bound by Printing Express Ltd, Hong Kong

Picture credits
Front cover: (background) sjt photographic/Alamy; (left) City of London; (bottom) The Mansell Collection; Back cover and spine: (back cover, centre) INSADCO Photography/Alamy; all other photography by Amanda Stanley

Contents

Introduction

THIS IS a different kind of book about churches and cathedrals. We hope that you will use it as a guide on your next visit to one of these fascinating buildings so that you can identify easily the important parts of the building and their function. But this is intended to be read as an unfolding story that opens before you a sense of the extraordinary richness of church architecture and history.

In some ways, discovering churches for the first time is like learning a language. In order to feel truly comfortable with your new skill you need not only to be aware of the facts: you need also a general understanding of local idiom and culture, and, beyond that, of the relevance and relationship of the subject to society as a whole. To encapsulate all this fully within the covers of a small book would be impossible. What can be done, however, is to present a sense of the significance of what can easily be found in almost any church, large or small and old or new. The important thing is that you as an enthusiast become aware of what tremendous potential this subject has for anyone with an interest in architecture and social history. You will discover how easy it can be to become 'fluent' in this fascinating and valuable area, and how it can become the basis of a highly enjoyable hobby.

For most of our history the parish church has been the dominant building in our villages and towns. Today these structures are only very rarely full of worshippers, and some have even been converted for other uses. Others are under threat, or have been demolished. Life for all of us has changed so much over the last 100 years that it might not be obvious why churches were once so important to every European community, and why their architecture and the details of their design have been so significant to our cultural history.

There was a time when all local government centred on the church. The minister of religion – a vicar or a rector in the Anglican Church, or a priest in Roman Catholic countries – was a central figure in the local population, and played an active part in its decisions. In all European nations, a position in a parish church might well have been an important stepping stone to a career in national politics. During the long period of religious revival in the early nineteenth century talented and hard-working young men were attracted to a life in the Church, and made it a power-house for social reform in their villages. Even now that elected politics and secular constitutions have long replaced ecclesiastical rule, the Church can still provide an important platform for campaigners and thinkers.

For these reasons, the Church has long been important as a social institution. In fact at times churches were built in large quantities in a single town because they were seen as an indispensable part of life. In the seaside resort city of Brighton an astonishing number of beautiful churches went up during the Victorian era, and our photographer, Amanda Stanley, has taken many photographs for this book there as a record of their outstanding quality and variety. For most churches are important as architecture, too. In the mediaeval village, a tower or a spire would have been the most imposing landmark for miles around, and the larger cities must have looked like a forest of pinnacles to travellers who approached them. These structures were built to impress with whatever means were available by architects and builders who knew how to exploit both local materials and, at times, an unparalleled level of craftsmanship.

Although some modern churches may seem very different from traditional ones, they are built to house ceremonies that have changed little in essentials for two thousand years. The early Christians developed a model for worship that has been carefully refined across all denominations throughout history, and in any church today it is easy to trace some ancient ideas and practices. At the same time, these buildings often used the most sophisticated contemporary design ideas, and they were built intentionally to be imposing and dignified. It is extraordinary, too, that churches generally contain the finest examples of every type of applied design, from painting to sculpture, from tiles to metalwork, and from stained glass to decorative joinery. Even the smallest pieces of ornament and decoration have a story to them.

In some cases a visitor can learn a great deal about a community by studying the details of what they see around them inside a church, or in its churchyard. The names and dates of ministers, benefactors and parishioners are often recorded on tablets, windows, pews and headstones. In many cases, such inscriptions or effigies may be the most poetic memorial that these people ever had. Mixed with religious sculpture or painting from all periods, a church interior can be a poignant place.

The church liturgy requires changes in costume and decorations throughout the year, and there are often signs of parish activities that change with the seasons. It is thanks to such traditions as much as to their varied architecture that our cathedrals and churches are the treasure houses of our cities and villages – and it is unlikely that there is any other building type which has so much to give to the visitor, and so much to say about local history and people's lives. Wherever you go with this book in your hand, you will soon discover that there is always a great deal more to a church than just a building.

Throughout this book you will find words in grey bold type on their first appearance. This indicates a word or phrase you are likely to encounter or need in a typical parish church. You can find short definitions for all of these words in the glossary at the end of the book.

CHAPTER ONE

The church and the village

THE MOMENT you step into any church you are confronted with hundreds of years of history. That is true, paradoxically, even of a modern church building. The explanation for this is that the design and layout of churches and the various activities associated with them have developed side by side with our religion, culture and politics.

LEFT Holy Trinity church from the river, Stratford-on-Avon, Warwickshire.

On entering a church

THIS BOOK is your guide to the richness of church architecture and history, and of the symbolism that you will encounter in any church building. That is not to say that you need to be an expert in order to enjoy much of what you see. Many people derive great pleasure from simply visiting historic churches, and this book's aim, first and foremost, is to enhance that pleasure by suggesting what features you might like to look out for and what their significance could be.

What is however important whenever passing through a lychgate at the edge of the churchyard, or entering the building through an ancient south porch, is to be aware of quite how much information there is around you. Much of that is specifically architectural, or to do with the location or layout of the building. But that is not all: there is a great deal going on that you cannot actually 'read' with your own eyes.

This is because the church both as a structure and as an establishment is deeply rooted in English social and political history. The people who built it and those that have served in it as rectors or vicars are part of a continuing history that has touched almost every detail of village life. So the first thing to be aware of when entering the church is what exactly the status of this institution is, and has been; and what the social significance was of the various church officers who have worked there.

The church at the centre of the village

For centuries the church stood at the centre of all everyday transactions. The idea that our needs as citizens should be organized and controlled centrally from a place far away is a modern one. For most of our history the average citizen had no direct dealings with any national or regional state authority at all, beyond the possibility of service in the army or navy – unless he or she got into serious trouble, in which case they might face a county judge. Everything they needed could be found close to hand. The only place where they might appear on an official list of any kind was in their church, where, for a significant period in its history, regular attendance was compulsory. The church was the centre of all public activity, and the rector or vicar, although in fact a member of a state organization and its representative locally, had considerable personal power to manage local affairs.

Understanding the historic location of the church and church land, and the pastoral and civic role of the man who presided over them, teaches us a great deal about what life was like at least as far as the end of the nineteenth century. The Anglo-Saxon and mediaeval division of the whole of the country into tiny units called parishes, each with its own church, tells us who controlled the land and what happened to its resources. And the records of the rector or vicar in the church are the stories of everyday lives of the people who lived there. The various buildings on church lands are themselves also documents of another kind, because of the way in which they reflect the changing interests and fortunes of an area. And so understanding the scope of the church's activities is always the first stage in discovering the true significance of what the great church buildings stand for.

The church is nearly always the focal point of the typical English village scene.

A remarkable and evocative Anglo-Saxon survival

All Saints, Earls Barton, Northamptonshire

LUCKILY for church enthusiasts, there are several largely complete Anglo-Saxon churches in existence in England as well as fragments of many more. All Saints, Earls Barton, is mainly a Norman church but its most distinctive feature is its tenth-century West tower. There may at first have been a small apse attached to it; it is impossible now to be sure. Although a parapet was added at the top in the fifteenth century, it remains one of the most startling and haunting pieces of pre-Norman Conquest architecture.

Part of the excitement of so early a church as this derives from a sense that the masons who built it were engaged in a series of delightful experiments that led to the creation of a truly English way of building. Look closely at the details of the exterior. Running up the full height of the corners is an example of the 'long-and-short-work' characteristic of Anglo-Saxon architecture: a sequence of a tall narrow stone followed by a short wide one. Other strips of stone called lesenes divide the rest of the tower, and at the third storey they form a pretty diamond pattern – a reminder that the Anglo-Saxons often used a simple triangular shape instead of an arch. The decorated window openings are supported by unusual bulging columns.

At Brixworth in the same county you can see a largely complete Anglo-Saxon church, and another well-known example was discovered at Bradford-on-Avon in Wiltshire in the mid-nineteenth century. The tower at Earls Barton is, however, special in its own right. With its fine and unusual detailing it gives a vivid picture of what an imposing Anglo-Saxon building looked like. And the exact meaning of its curious decoration and openings will remain forever a mystery.

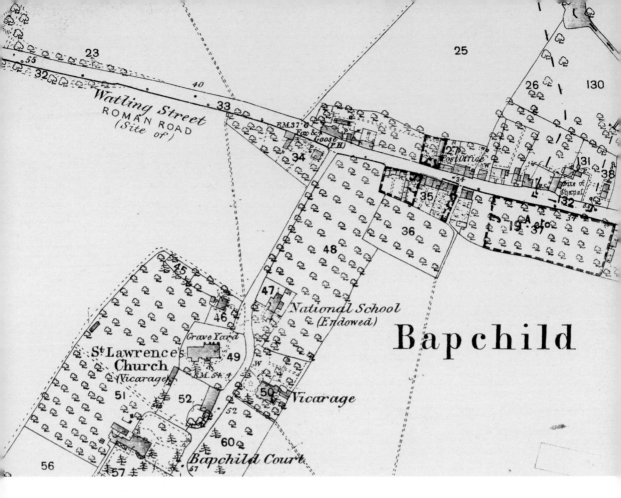

The Church and the churches

The church and its churchyard usually lie at the heart of the village. This is an extract enlarged from a first edition Ordnance Survey map of 1872.

The Church with a capital 'C' is an institution: a large, often national or international organization that exists mainly to promote the doctrine of Jesus Christ. A church with a lower-case 'c' is a building in which the Church can do the part of its work that requires a permanent location. The Churches of different countries have naturally developed architecturally, as well as socially or politically, in varying ways; even an international Church, such as the Roman Catholic Church, will often have a distinct architectural character to it in a certain country.

This book will start by looking at the Church of England, the national Church institution of the country. It is that profound link between the Church of England and the state that has created the special importance that churches have to all national and local history. But, as we shall see, the other Churches have an important role to play too.

The church and the parish

SOME OF THE terminology of the Church of England is a little confusing because it developed slowly over the centuries; furthermore, many areas have built up unusual conventions of their own. But recognizing the basic names and titles is important, because it opens before us the world of church histories and records.

The parish

The parish is the building block of English local history. The word does, however, have no fewer than three distinct meanings. All of them refer to the area around a church, usually including a single village, town, or part of a city.

One meaning of the word 'parish' is purely modern and civic: it is an area that has an elected council that is responsible for some activities such as maintaining local public property such as halls or bus shelters.

The second meaning is the modern descendant of an ancient forbearer: it is a broad term for the places and activities that come under the responsibility of what is today called a parochial church council (PCC). This is a small committee chaired by the incumbent (see page 18) and with elected members, called churchwardens; legally it owns and is responsible for the church building and churchyard. The 'parish' in this sense also includes by implication those who do, or might, attend services in the church nearest to where they live.

The PCC and the modern civic parish are both derived from the old historical parish and it is the parish in this third sense that provides the framework for so much of our social and local history from earliest times and right up to the end of the Victorian era. The boundaries of these historical parishes may be similar or even identical to those of the modern parishes. The historical parish was, originally, a division of land defined perhaps as long ago as Anglo-Saxon times, before the Norman Conquest of 1066. The boundaries of parishes did change from time to time, and many new parishes were carved out from old ones during the period of church growth in the nineteenth century; in general, however, it is surprising how ancient these boundaries can be.

This historical parish was, through the centuries, increasingly responsible for nearly all the services that we now think of as 'public': road repairs, street lighting, even the care of miscreants, the unemployed and the sick. In time these responsibilities were taken over by new and generally much larger authorities. In London, for example, the parishes, some of them recently formed ones, already had comparatively few functions by the time a central authority for controlling new building and infrastructure, called the Metropolitan Board of Works, was established in 1855. To some extent they survived as units of local government until as late as 1900. In the rest of England the civic duties of ecclesiastical parishes were reformed during the course of the nineteenth century, and the modern civic parish was introduced in 1894.

In general the historical parish was controlled by a group named after the room they met in: the vestry.

The vestry

The vestry is a room usually near the eastern end of a church where the person conducting a service puts on their robes. Because it was often the only convenient small room in a church, it was traditionally the meeting place for the group of people who were responsible for parish affairs in the days when the parish was still the local unit of government.

These people consisted of the church incumbent and various others – the exact number varying by tradition from place to place. Together they formed the group known itself as 'the vestry'. Some of these were open vestries, which meant that meetings were more or less open to all ratepayers; others were select vestries, which meant that attendance was restricted.

The incumbent

The correct general term for someone known as the parish priest, rector or vicar is the incumbent – a word almost never used in normal conversation. It is however a useful term when writing about local history because all the other expressions traditionally had different and distinct meanings. In old-fashioned usage an incumbent was also known as a parson. In order to make it clear when this book is referring only to a historical situation, the word 'parson' will be used.

In today's Church of England, it makes no difference whether the incumbent is called 'vicar' or 'rector', although when a group of ministers is appointed to a team ministry to work together across several parishes that have been merged together for church administrative purposes, the head of that team is called a 'rector' to distinguish him or her from the others in the team. The term curate is generally used today to mean an assistant to the incumbent.

The Reformation

THE REFORMATION is the central event in English Church history. The Western Church had since its foundation been controlled by the pope, the bishop of Rome. On many occasions since the establishment of the mediaeval Church, an English king had found himself opposing the power of the pope. Sometimes this was because of financial demands the pope made on the English taxpayers in order to support the Church, and sometimes it was because the pope disapproved of a particular action by the king.

The Reformation is the name given to the process whereby the English branch of the Church first became independent of Rome, and secondly transformed itself into a Protestant Church that rejected several beliefs and practices of the Western Church controlled by the pope.

The first stage occurred in 1533 when King Henry VIII of England, who ruled between 1509 and 1547, was

The German priest and theologian Martin Luther (1483–1546) is considered to be the father of the Protestant revolution. Here, Luther is shown burning the papal bull.

refused permission by Pope Clement VII to divorce his first wife, Catherine of Aragon, and to marry Anne Boleyn. The king decided to reject the pope's authority and ordered Thomas Cranmer, the new Archbishop of Canterbury, to permit the divorce and remarriage; the following year the king proclaimed himself head of the Church in England. In this position he closed down many monasteries and other Church institutions, usually taking or selling their land and with it their rights of patronage and their income from agriculture and rents. In effect, he 'nationalized' the English Church.

The second stage occurred mainly during the reign of Henry's young son Edward VI (1547–53). Cranmer led the English Church through a period of theological reform, adopting a position similar to that called for by Martin Luther in Germany which is known as Protestantism. Some traditions of Christianity as it was practised by the pope – henceforth known by the name Roman Catholicism – were forbidden. These were mainly the more mystical practices, but also others that involved money and had fallen into disrepute. In 1549 Cranmer published a new Book of Common Prayer, in English rather than the traditional Latin, that was to form the basis of the liturgy of the reformed Church.

The brief reign of Edward's sister Mary saw an attempt to return to Roman Catholicism, but her sister Elizabeth, who became queen in 1558, restored the independence and legal status of the English Church while resisting the attempts of reformers to revert to the more strictly Protestant theology of the days of Edward VI. In 1563 the Church published the Thirty-Nine Articles, the basic religious tenets of what is today called Anglicanism. Her nephew and successor King James VI of Scotland and I of England, who was himself a Protestant, ordered a new translation of the Bible known as the Authorised Version to be used in Anglican churches. The final significant stage in the creation of the identity of the Church of England was the publication of the widely used and much loved new Book of Common Prayer of 1662.

The early history of the Church of England involved as much politics as theology: Britain was constantly under military threat from major Roman Catholic powers such as Spain and France, and consequently the insistence on the primacy of the English Church was an important ingredient in developing a proud national identity.

As sure as I am Parson Puzzle-Text they have clapp'd me up in the Print Shops.. I have a great mind to break the windows.

Don't be angry Neighbour.. you should not be suprised at any thing in London! why look ye there I declare they have got me too.. in my Volunteer Uniform— but see how quietly I take it " they like to see people in a passion —!

The parson (left) has often been a figure of fascination and ridicule among satirists.

The patron

The patron is the person or institution who is responsible for recommending a candidate for the position of incumbent of a parish church. Sometimes this is a local landowner; sometimes it is a body such as an Oxford or Cambridge college that succeeded to the right of patronage from a monastic foundation after the Reformation (see pages 19–20).

The holding of a parish by an incumbent is called a benefice or a living, to which the patron is said to 'present' their candidate. The appointment has to be approved by the local bishop, so sometimes it is a matter of tactful negotiation. In practice nowadays the bishop very often consults the patron, rather than the other way around. The bishop can himself be a patron, as can the Crown.

The right to present someone to a living is known historically as an advowson – a commodity related to the ownership of land and which until relatively recently could be inherited, bought or sold.

Rector or vicar?

The difference between the status of a rector and a vicar is one that has puzzled many people. It is important to emphasize that the difference between the two titles is an historical one and has no bearing on the present-day holders of the title. But it may be helpful to describe in general terms the historical distinction between the two positions.

This distinction was based on their source of income. A parson's income came from a tax on local agricultural produce that was known as the tithes. These were composed mainly of two types of tax: the little tithes and the great tithes. As a rule of thumb, the little tithes were a proportion of everything grown *on* the land: small animals such as sheep and goats, for example, but also of some small plant produce such as fruit trees and vegetables. The great tithes were historically a tax of everything grown *in* the land, such as grains like wheat and barley, but also of large farm animals. The concept of a tithe is a biblical one, and it meant ten per cent of the total produce.

Every parish had a rector, but that rector was not necessarily acting as the parson. If the rector was an acting parson, he received both great and little tithes. If the rector was elsewhere, the great tithes still had to be paid to him and a vicar was appointed to do the day-to-day work of the parson. The vicar received an income either in the form of the little tithes, or in the form of a salary from the theoretical rector derived from the value of the little tithes.

From this it can be seen that a rector was historically a more prestigious person than a vicar. He may have been treated as such socially and lived in a bigger or better house. And yet a vicar in a rich agricultural part of the country would be likely to have had a better quality of life than a rector in a poor one.

Incidentally, the rectorship of a parish where a vicar had been installed actually to do the work of the parson could well pass into non-church hands. A person holding this kind of rectorship is called a lay rector. They still exist – and some of them have unexpectedly found themselves responsible for paying for the upkeep or repair of their local church.

As for today's rector or vicar – they both receive a salary directly from the Church, which ceased to collect tithes in any form in 1936.

Who is who in the Church of England?

- THE **monarch** is the head of the Church of England.
- The **Archbishop of Canterbury** is the Primate of All England, and head of the Anglican communion worldwide. He resides officially at Lambeth Palace in London and is a member of the House of Lords and the Privy Council. He retains these two latter positions after his retirement from office.
- The **Archbishop of York** is the second most senior clergyman in the Church of England. He too is a member of the House of Lords.
- A **diocesan bishop** is one of a group of senior clergymen. He is based at a cathedral which is located in his diocese – the area for which he is responsible for a number of tasks such as ordaining new clergy and appointing them to livings. Twenty-four diocesan bishops are also members of the House of Lords at any one time.
- A **suffragan bishop** is a deputy to the diocesan bishop, with responsibility for a particular area within the diocese.
- An **archdeacon** is a senior clergyman with responsibility for inspecting and reporting on parishes in a diocese. Archdeacons can carry out some of the diocesan responsibilities of a bishop on his behalf. The area for which the archdeacon is responsible is called an archdeaconry. The populous Diocese of London has six archdeaconries.
- A **dean** is the senior clergyman responsible for the running of a cathedral. In matters concerning the fabric and management of the cathedral itself, he takes precedence (in practice, at any rate) over the bishop. He is head of the cathedral chapter – the officers and canons attached to the building.
- A **rural dean** is an incumbent with special responsibility for a group of parishes called a 'deanery'. He will be required to keep the bishop updated with events in the parishes, usually through the offices of the archdeacon.
- A **canon** is a priest, usually also nowadays an incumbent, who is a member of the cathedral chapter.

A procession of clergy and nobility, 1512. The figures are wearing ceremonial robes and carrying symbols of office.

- **A prebendary** is today an honorary title given to a clergyman.
- **A chaplain** is a priest attached to an institution (such as a college) or, historically, to a family.
- **Priest** and **clergyman** are the general terms for ordained people.
- An **incumbent** is the general name for the rector or the vicar of a parish.
- **A parson** is an old name for an incumbent.
- **A priest in charge** is a new name for an incumbent, favoured in some places.
- **A rector** historically received the great tithes.
- **A vicar** historically received the little tithes.
- **A curate**, which is really an abbreviation for 'assistant curate', was and is an assistant to an incumbent.
- An **assistant priest** is an ordained assistant curate. These two titles are not exactly interchangeable, and their use varies from parish to parish.
- **A team ministry**, headed by a rector, is a group of priests appointed to run several parishes together.
- **A deacon** is a layperson who is not or not yet ordained and who assists the incumbent and is permitted to carry out some of the duties of an ordained priest.
- **A churchwarden** is one of two members of a parochial church council annually elected by parishioners.
- The **congregation** are people who live in the parish and attend services.

The curate

The curate today is an assistant to the incumbent, but the title of curate has also had a role in English church history across the generations. It has often been rather a sad one. This is because he had little right to any reasonable fixed income at all: he was dependent on his incumbent to pay a salary, which could be very little. Historically, a curate might have had to carry out all the work of the incumbent (who could well have been living some distance away) and yet still have very little in the way of security or comfort. There is a great deal of eighteenth-century literature bemoaning the lot of the poor curate, and it was only during a period of church administration reform in the early nineteenth century that any fixed income, albeit small, could be promised.

Any clergyman without good social or family connections might have ended up as a curate for a good long period, or perhaps for the whole of his life, because he was never presented to a living in his own right. Getting that living was the fundamental breakthrough in a church career – which is why novelists such as Jane Austen, writing in the early nineteenth century, attached such importance to it happening to their characters.

Parsons, such as Mr Elton in *Emma*, are familiar figures in Jane Austen's novels.

The Church as a record of England

THE CHURCH and its parson provided for many people in earlier times a great deal of certainty in life. A vicar or rector might stay in a parish for the whole of their adult life, devoting decades to its people. By the time of the later Middle Ages, a clergyman was also an educated person, and would have studied at Oxford or Cambridge, universities which were in effect religious institutions and whose primary purpose was to educate people for the priesthood.

The parson was therefore the logical person to act as registrar for personal and ceremonial events in a village. For centuries he might well have been the only person in the vicinity, but for a few educated landowners, who could read or write. He was authorized to carry out baptisms, weddings and funerals, and since the Church of England was the state Church, he did this – as indeed all incumbents still do – as an agent of the state, without requiring further approval by a lay official. Since he would be likely to know most, if not all, of his parishioners by name, and since until recent times most of them attended church regularly, he would have been able to verify people's identities and would have known, for example, whether a person was eligible for marriage or not. The records he kept of all these activities in his parish are therefore the bedrock of English demographic history.

In 1837 the United Kingdom government passed an act of parliament which allowed civil weddings to take place without the presence of a clergyman. From this point onwards, the local registers of a parish begin to decrease in importance. Political and social changes in the country as a whole also altered the way, and the place, in which these details of social history were recorded. The Churches outside the Church of England, which were liberated from most of the legal restrictions put on them at around this time, additionally began to maintain records of their members and the ceremonies enacted between them. But the parish registers of England still provide a remarkable record of daily parish life, and are of vital interest to those tracing the lives of their ancestors. Most of them are now part of diocesan archives, which often form separate collections in county record offices.

Other types of parish record are also of great interest to local and family historians. Most parishes kept a chest for records recording transactions, including correspondence of all kinds and vestry decisions on those unfortunate individuals who came in need of help or misbehaved; some parsons even placed there a kind of journal which can reveal details of life in the village.

Because of the important role that the tithes paid in the life of the church, maps were drawn up to show land ownership. Some of these tithe maps are very ancient and can be found today in diocesan collections.

A further type of parish record is the terrier – a word derived from the Latin word *terra*, meaning earth. A terrier is a survey of land and an inventory of all the property, moveable or fixed, on it. In order to protect the interests of incumbents, all parishes were first required by an act of parliament in 1571 to submit these terriers to their local bishop for safekeeping. Historical terriers, too, can be found in the various diocesan record collections.

The parish chest was the traditional repository for papers recording important local decisions and transactions. Some old ones survive.

Diaries and correspondence

There is a further, informal, source of information about life in an English parish that is worth bearing in mind: the diaries and correspondence of literary-minded parsons. One of the most remarkable of these was Francis Kilvert, a poor clergyman in rural Wales who wrote movingly about his life there and the people he encountered until his early death in 1879. Patrick Brontë, the father of Charlotte, Emily and Anne, was the perpetual curate at Haworth in Yorkshire from 1820 until his death in 1861, outliving all his daughters; an eccentric but literary man of modest origins and with a wealth of harsh personal experience, his letters breathe life into the rigours of daily life in a far-flung parish.

LEFT
Patrick Brontë, the father of novelists Charlotte, Emily and Anne, was a prolific correspondent whose letters record parish life.

RIGHT
The diarist Francis Kilvert wrote movingly and evocatively about life in a rural Welsh parish in the 1870s.

The church and the village

Colourful clergy

MANY PARSONS throughout history have been remarkable and colourful characters. Here are three of the best known.

The rector of Stiffkey

Stiffkey, often pronounced 'stooky', is a small village on the north coast of Norfolk. In 1906 Harold Davidson became its rector. Soon after his appointment and all through the 1920s he devoted a great deal of his time to the streets of London, far from his parishioners, engaged in mission work and befriending young girls in the hope of rescuing them from a life of sin. Not everyone was sympathetic to Davidson's explanations as to why he spent so much time with these girls, and the result was that he eventually found himself facing an ecclesiastical court. Following a salacious trial in 1932 he was found guilty on several counts of immoral conduct. Inevitably he was defrocked – stripped of his rights as a priest – in a rowdy ceremony in Norwich cathedral.

Davidson's story is the more dramatic for its terrible end. Driven to making a living as a fairground attraction, he was fatally mauled by a lion in Skegness Amusement Park and died in 1937.

Richard Waldo Sibthorp

Perhaps the epitome of the pious Victorian who was obsessed by finding religious fulfilment, Richard Waldo Sibthorp was a tragic character of a different kind. He moved several times between Anglicanism and Roman Catholicism in a fruitless search for peace of mind, each time losing both friends and career prospects.

Born in 1792 into an Anglican family, he tried to convert to Catholicism as a student but was prevented by his family from doing so at the last minute. He first became an evangelical priest, but after a process of becoming increasingly eccentric in his ways, he became a Catholic in 1841– an event much trumpeted by the fast-growing Catholic community in England. Two years later, and following a serious accident, he returned to the Church of England. In 1865 he became a Catholic again – but his funeral service was held according to the Anglican rites. A kindly and lonely figure, for many he symbolized the dangers of obsessive religiosity and lack of moral steadfastness.

Sydney Smith
On the other hand, Sydney Smith, born in 1771, was quite a different sort of character. He was obliged by family circumstances to enter the Church, and at first he found both the prospect and the actuality of a small remote parish immensely boring. He was a large, witty, sociable man with plenty of friends in London; but to his horror he was eventually obliged to move to his living, Foston-le-Clay near York, by new legislation that was aimed at keeping parsons in their parishes. Here he built himself a large house to his own design, and forced himself to become acquainted with country life.

Smith was a prolific writer and the source of many amusing stories told by his well-connected friends in London.

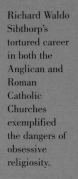

Richard Waldo Sibthorp's tortured career in both the Anglican and Roman Catholic Churches exemplified the dangers of obsessive religiosity.

Church premises

THE INFLUENCE of the church and its incumbent extended far beyond the walls of the church and churchyard. As you would expect from his central role in the village, the parson was responsible for rather more than just a single building. Here are a number of other important features of the historical and present-day life of the parish:

The parsonage

Traditionally, the rectory or vicarage has always belonged to the incumbent: ownership comes with the job, and on leaving, retirement, or death, the house passes over to the newcomer. It is the incumbent's responsibility to keep the house in good order.

Vicarages and rectories were often impressive buildings and their style reflected the architectural fashions of the period in which they were built.

Until the mid-nineteenth century, not every parish had a parsonage because a parson might well have had more than one living; he would live in the one he preferred, or indeed somewhere else altogether. He might have had to provide a home for the curate who operated in a living on his behalf, but many did not bother. The comparative poverty of much of clerical life in the eighteenth century, the legislation that limited its funding, and the detachment of senior churchmen from the practical problems of their juniors all combined to create a situation whereby there were not enough houses for the clergy in thousands of parishes in England, and many of the buildings that did exist were in a dire state of decay. The few grand old parsonages of this period are generally a sign that there was a generous patron, or alternatively a parson with a private income. In the early nineteenth century, when a religious revival swept the country and as the junior sons of the gentry took up a career in the Church in substantial numbers, legislation both insisted that clergymen committed themselves to a single parish and also enabled them to apply for a mortgage on favourable terms in order to live there in reasonable comfort.

One interesting result of this latter legislation is that we have a great number of detailed records about the building of new parsonages in the late Georgian and early Victorian eras, and this provides us with a wonderful picture of how their architecture began to change as the gothic revival swept across the country. These records are in the diocesan collections. The new houses were often substantial and well equipped with modern conveniences: many parsons had large families requiring perhaps six or seven bedrooms, and rooms for servants. These big houses have generally been sold off by the Church over the course of the second half of the twentieth century and they can be recognized by their names: 'The Old Rectory', or 'The Old Vicarage'. Sometimes even the replacement house became too large in its turn, and a yet smaller one was built. In these circumstances you might find not only 'The Rectory' (where the incumbent now lives) but also both 'The Old Rectory' and 'Rectory House'.

Incidentally, a living that had a rector was traditionally itself called 'a rectory' and that with a vicar 'a vicarage' – so when you see this term in old documents and maps the reference is most likely to the status of the parish as a whole and not to a building. At that time people referred to the parson's residence itself as 'the rectory house' or the 'vicarage house'.

The church and the village

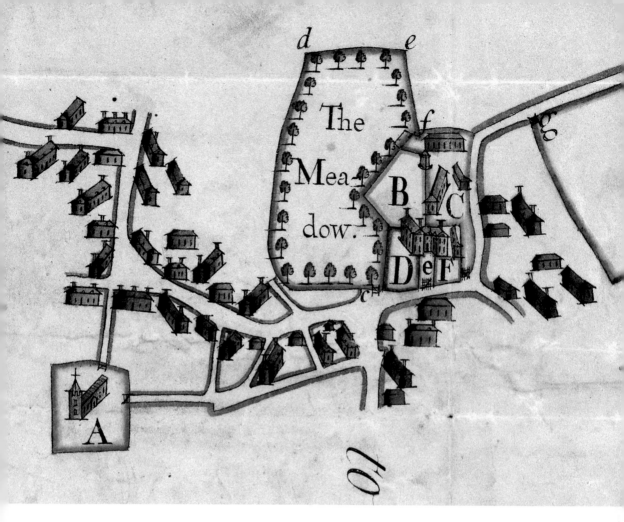

The glebe

The glebe was traditionally land in parish ownership; the parsonage was built on it, and it provided the parson with an income either through letting the land or farming it himself. Glebe terriers often document their history. Today glebe land belongs to the local diocese, which can develop it or lease it according to the policy of the church.

In addition to these diocesan glebe lands, the Church of England owns property nationally which has over the centuries been accumulated from different sources. It is managed by the Church Commissioners in London, with profits returned to the running of the church. As with many large national organizations, the Church is increasingly under pressure to meet its pension commitments and consequently its property needs to be managed in a profitable way similar to that of any other investment.

The village of West Meon as depicted on a beautiful glebe terrier of 1758 (Hampshire Record Office, 21M65/E15/120).

The tithe barn

Originally the tithe payments which supported the church were simply paid by handing over a tenth of the produce directly to the parson: if a farmer bred ten chickens, he brought one along to the parsonage. There were other forms of payment in the form of agricultural produce to which some parsons were also entitled. All this required considerable storage space, in particular where a rector was in receipt of large amounts of grain.

For this reason many parishes had substantial barns for collecting all the produce, similar to (although smaller than) some of the great barns of the monasteries which likewise depended on the fortunes of local agriculture. The obvious inconvenience of collecting and storing the produce resulted in a process – a very slow one, as is usually the case with reforms in Church traditions – of converting or 'commuting' the tithes into fixed cash payments. The barn could then be let by the parson to a farmer in order to provide further income – until it eventually fell down.

Rectorial tithe barns have largely disappeared. This surviving fifteenth-century one at Nailsea, North Somerset, has been converted into a community hall.

The village school

Until 1870 the provision of primary school education in England was a matter of chance: in some places voluntary organizations provided a decent school, and in other places no one did. At all events an active vestry, headed by the local parson, could build a school and promote education and literacy. An Anglican organization called the National Society was founded in 1811 in order to promote the building of church schools of this kind. Thousands were erected in the early and mid-nineteenth century when church attendance was growing, and many of these structures can still be found. Some of these schools were run by the parson's wife, and the larger Victorian parsonages incorporated a schoolroom.

Until the days of universal state provision local schools were often built under the private patronage of the parson or with Church funds.

The almshouse and the workhouse

The vestry distributed money to the poor and needy, and sometimes built homes for them. Many old almshouses are actually the result of a private benefaction, but the

The parson and the vestry were sometimes trustees of charitable local almshouses built by private benefactors to house the village elderly. These ones in Fulham are beside the parish church.

vestry members might have been its trustees or owners. Building a workhouse to provide shelter for those incapable of working was not, however, the type of project to attract an endowment from a wealthy landowner, so vestries were required to build these themselves.

Early workhouses were not necessarily forbidding buildings; they are usually on a small scale since they were intended to provide only for the local poor. Indeed, it was during certain periods illegal to seek any kind of poor relief, as public financial assistance or shelter was called, from a parish other than your own. But the small parish workhouses could not cope with the mass migration into the towns and cities from the Industrial Revolution onwards. In 1834 an act of parliament set up larger unions – joint parish boards – to replace local vestry control and build the widely despised prison-like structures which have become infamous from novels like Charles Dickens' *Oliver Twist*. This process is an example of the way the civil powers of the parish were taken over by ever-more centralized bodies over the course of the nineteenth century.

This former workhouse at Nantwich, Cheshire, constructed in 1780, is today used as offices.

The Church calendar

UNLIKE the civil or Gregorian calendar year, which begins on the first of January, the Church's year begins in the late autumn with the lead up to Christmas. It is divided into seasons instead of months, and starts on the first Sunday in Advent.

- Advent
- Christmas
- Epiphany
- Lent
- Easter

Periods between these seasons are named Ordinary Time, and much of the long period between Easter and Advent is referred to by the number of weeks following Trinity Sunday.

Church dates are fixed by a different method from civil ones and therefore they coincide with monthly dates that change from year to year. This is because some significant Christian festivals are derived from Jewish ones. For example, the timing of Easter is derived from Passover, when Jesus participated in the traditional feast before his arrest. The first day of Passover is always the 15th of Nissan according to the Hebrew calendar, but the Hebrew year is shorter than the Gregorian one and is adjusted to suit the seasons by an occasional extra month. As the date of Passover varies on the Gregorian calendar, so does Easter.

Festivals in the Church calendar were often used in civil life, for example as completion dates in building contracts. The academic year, running from September to June, has its roots in church traditions.

Saints' days were used instead of civil dates by the mediaeval church, and still have a significant role to play in the calendar used by the Roman Catholic Church.

A detail from a mediaeval table for calculating the date of Easter, kept by the monks of Christ Church, Canterbury.

The parish and the parson in English culture

IT CAN readily be seen that the English parish, with its church, its parson, and its various interests and responsibilities made up a central part of English life, especially since before the mid-nineteenth century most people lived in rural areas under the watchful eye of the village church. It is therefore not surprising that churches and their parsons have a major role to play in English art and literature too.

Paintings

In some cases artists could sum up the character of a landscape by painting a church at the centre of their composition. In 1814 the well-known landscape painter John Constable created a famous view of the River Stour with the church of the Essex village of Dedham as a focal point. This painting is in the Boston Museum of Fine Art in the United States, where for many it must sum up the English landscape at its most picturesque and beautiful. In part this is due to the striking and memorable nature of the church building; but it is also because this type of composition inevitably displays a very English character, capturing the village architecture of England at its most evocative. Filmmakers likewise often use distant views of village churches, surrounded by cottages and fields, to establish an immediate sense of English village life. By way

John Constable's paintings of Dedham Vale focus on the spire of the local village church. This early version dates from 1802.

For early Victorian artists and writers, depicting a church was a way of representing the positive values of Christianity. This is the concluding illustration from Dickens' *Nicholas Nickleby*.

of comparison, Dutch artists of the sixteenth and seventeenth centuries created many thousands of detailed painted views of the inside of their churches, and these too have come to be for most of us an image of the true nature of these buildings and the people who used them.

Victorian illustrators liked to use an image of a church in order to conjure up a picture of respectable and secure happiness: the closing illustration to Charles Dickens' *Nicholas Nickleby* is one of these. In fact Dickens' early novels, written at the time that the Church nationally was growing in importance, make a great deal of use of churches both in words and pictures to convey simple moral messages.

Novels

For similar reasons parsons crop up regularly in English literature, especially around the first half of the nineteenth century. Reading these books now gives a wonderful picture of the way in which village life was changing in Britain.

Jane Austen, herself the daughter of the rector of Steventon in Hampshire, included clergymen in most of her novels which were written in the period between about 1800 and her death in 1817. It is very remarkable how little attention these men seem to pay to the everyday work of the parish; the religious revival was yet to happen, and many were content to live comfortable lives often far from their parishioners. Mr Tilney in *Northanger Abbey* is the son of the patron of the living, at whose expense he has been fitted up with a comfortable new house; however he spends only about half his time there, for his father's mansion nearly 20 miles away is a great deal bigger and more comfortable still. Mr Collins, in *Pride and Prejudice*, is only 25 years old but already 'grave and stately'. Edmund Bertram in *Mansfield Park* is similarly a highly serious young man; but Mr Elton in *Emma* is rather a clown (see the picture on page 25). His residence in one of the modest, unimproved vicarages of the time makes a vivid contrast with the comfortable homes of the local gentry where he is a welcome visitor. Unusually for Austen's clergymen, he does at least conduct services from time to time.

The fictional parsons of Victorian literature tend on the other hand to be serious people with a strong sense of duty that comes at the expense of more easily likeable qualities, although some, like Anne Brontë's Mr Weston in *Agnes Grey*, do manage to combine the two. More realistic and far more memorable is George Eliot's *Scenes of Clerical Life*, which describes in painful detail the struggles of clergymen in poor parishes as the religious revival is taking place. Mr Gilfil is an old-fashioned, rather shy clergyman who presides over a decaying church; Amos Barton, coming to the parish as a poor curate some years later, is an unlikeable but persistent character who too late wins the hearts of his parishioners. And the clergyman of the third tale in the book, Edgar Tryan, is a modern, evangelical minister of the kind that the religious revival was built on. Characters in novels are not generally supposed to be understood as real, historical people, and yet figures such as these really can illuminate the role and character of the Church at critical times in its history.

The novelist best known for his portrayal of clerical figures is Anthony Trollope, who wrote a series of six novels set in an imaginary county called Barsetshire and in particular around Barchester cathedral, a place dominated by the stern, alarming figure of Archdeacon Grantly, one of several characters who appear in all the novels. These books are filled with parsons of all kinds; they are mostly slightly ridiculous, appearing here by way of mild satire on a way of life that Trollope knew well. A distant family member of Trollope's, the novelist Joanna Trollope, has continued his tradition by writing successful novels about the clergymen of the present day.

The church and the village

Famous churches in English history

IT IS NOT only the politics of the Church that have sometimes played a decisive role in English history; occasionally the buildings themselves have provided a backdrop to great events too. Perhaps the best known in this respect is the parish church of St Mary, Putney, which played host to a series of debates between leaders of the parliamentary faction in 1647 about the constitutional future of England. Among the participants were Oliver Cromwell and Henry Ireton, who strongly resisted calls from radicals to introduce universal suffrage. It was here that Colonel Thomas Rainborowe famously declared that 'the poorest he that is in England hath a life to live as the greatest he'. The debates were inconclusive – and Cromwell in any case eventually established an autocratic regime. Some parts of the old church tower still exist; much of the rest has been rebuilt.

A church that has seen many important events is the University Church of St Mary the Virgin in Oxford. During the reign of Mary I the trials of the Protestant bishops Hugh Latimer and Nicholas Ridley took place here, and Thomas Cranmer dramatically refused to recant his Protestant faith. All three were sentenced to death. In the nineteenth century the church again found itself at the centre of a storm of controversy when it provided a pulpit for the reformers who launched the Oxford Movement – the campaign to return English Protestantism to its spiritual mediaeval roots. It was largely thanks to this group of clergymen and the designers who rallied to their cause that the familiar Victorian gothic church with its splendid architecture and fittings became a common sight across the country.

The University Church of St Mary the Virgin, Oxford.

The most delightful of all Norman churches

St Mary and St David, Kilpeck, Herefordshire

THIS LITTLE red sandstone church has some of the most rewarding Norman carvings in England. The building, probably dating from the mid-twelfth century during the turbulent reign of King Stephen, is simple in form: it has a single-space nave, a chancel, and an apse. It is, however, merely the backdrop for some of the most remarkable early ornament to survive in this country.

The most magnificent of all Kilpeck's treasures is its splendid southern doorway. The tympanum — the semi-circular panel under the arch — displays a tree of life. Above and around it come a series of decorated arches. One of these has a series of carvings of monsters with an angel at their centre; and the outer one consists of a chain whose links contain elegant stylized birds. The columns either side of the door are carved with dragons, warriors with pointed hats, and foliage in a pattern that looks frankly Viking, and one of the impost mouldings takes the form of a face spewing tendrils. Nikolaus Pevsner wrote that the founder of the local priory had visited Santiago de Compostela in Spain, so possibly the inspiration for this decoration was drawn from far and wide.

The exterior also boasts a fine corbel table — a continuous horizontal projection supported by carved figures. Some of these look like modern children's cartoons. You can see a friendly dog and hare, a bear, a musician, and several comic and mythical creatures. And there is a very rude sheela-na-gig — the female carving commonly said to ward off evil spirits.

Step inside this church and the delights of Kilpeck continue: the simple whitewashed interior is enlivened by the two groups of sombre, elongated figures carved either side of the chancel arch.

Churches beyond the Church of England

The architecture of Roman Catholic churches in Britain sometimes has a Mediterranean appearance.

THE CHURCH of England is different from other Churches because of its central role in English social history and its intimate connection with village life. This situation was for centuries upheld by discriminatory laws in its favour, and these established its special rights in the lives of parishioners who had very little dealings with the few state authorities that did exist.

For politicians, the status of the national Church seemed to be vital in order to ensure the security and stability of the nation as a whole. This was often true even among those who did not much care for the Church and its ways – indeed, the eighteenth century is characterized on the one hand by a detached disdain by many politicians for clerical interests and yet a toughening stance against those who dissented from Anglican worship on the other. Roman Catholics were forbidden from worshipping in public places in Britain until 1791; they had to do so in secret, in private family chapels, or in chapels attached to foreign embassies in London. The first new Catholic chapel was probably that built at Newport, Isle of Wight, in the year the act was passed.

The position changed entirely during the eventful period of the early nineteenth century. It was very probably as a result of the British government's attempts to maintain its rule in Ireland that Roman Catholics throughout the kingdom were finally given civil rights equal to those of Anglicans, although even the passing of the Catholic Emancipation Act of 1829 still did not end discrimination in several respects. From that point on, however, Catholicism in Britain grew fast, aided by mass immigration from Ireland in the mid-nineteenth century. Many fine buildings were erected across the country and the new Catholic parishes and (from 1850) dioceses began to keep records similar to those of the Church of England.

The Roman Catholics became the largest group after the Anglicans, but they were only one group of several types of dissenters or nonconformists (as non-Anglicans of various kinds were known) to build distinctive churches. The religious fervour of nineteenth-century society provided a sympathetic audience to charismatic preachers and therefore it resulted in large new buildings in which to accommodate them. Baptists, Methodist groups of various types, Congregationalists and others built churches of their own, often grouped around particular geographical areas. The Quakers, a group with Christian origins and roots but not explicitly Christian in its worship, built not churches but meeting houses with a distinctive architecture of their own.

The large cities of the Midlands and the North of England developed wealthy nonconformist communities that funded impressive building programmes. The many fine new buildings paid for by these communities themselves testify very clearly to the way in which power and money were in England moving away from the landed aristocracy and into the towns and cities where most of the population now lived. Most of these religious groups survive in some form; some, such as the Catholic Apostolic Church, have faded away – leaving some dramatic church buildings behind in evidence of their short but glorious past which coincided with one of the most exciting periods in English architecture.

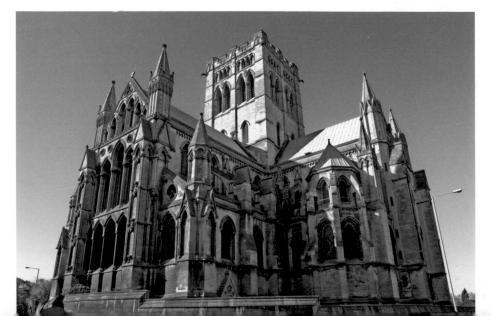

The Roman Catholic cathedral of St John the Baptist, Norwich.

The Anglican Church worldwide

THE CHURCH of England stands at the heart of a group of allied Churches throughout the world which are together known as the Anglican Communion.

Within the British Isles themselves, the way in which the common beliefs of the Church of England spread was highly dependent on the broader political situation. The Church of Scotland, a Presbyterian Church without bishops, was recognized as the established religion in Scotland when England and Scotland united in 1707, and thus the Anglican Church there has a less dominant presence. The Church of Wales was closely allied to the Church of England, and operated on a similar model but without parlia-mentary representation in the House of Lords. The Church of Ireland, however, was intended to be represen-tative of the ruling British Protestant state, and it enjoyed the rights of an established Church until the late nineteenth century even though the majority of the island's population was Roman Catholic.

The Anglican Communion world-wide originated with the spread of Britain's trading empire and people throughout the eighteenth and nineteenth centuries, for every British community living abroad brought along its own religious traditions. Today the local Anglican Churches, usually known as Episcopal (or Episcopalian) Churches, have large congregations across North America, Africa, and Australia and New Zealand, although none have the traditional relationship with the state that the Church of England has.

The bishops of the Anglican Communion meet regularly to discuss common policy, and they have estab-lished many joint international projects. The leader of the Anglican Communion is by tradition the Archbishop of Canterbury.

The Most Reverend Katharine Jefferts Schori is the Presiding Bishop and Primate of the Episcopal Church, based in the United States of America. She became the first Anglican woman primate in 2006.

Outside the parish – the Church and the nation

THE NEXT step is, perhaps surprisingly, to look at the great cathedrals of England. They may seem very different from the average parish church, and yet they are the key to understanding and describing the way these much smaller buildings work.

On the one hand their layout and style, magnificent as they are, provide memorable and easily legible examples of the way in which small gothic churches are designed. But secondly, they also are a reminder of the extent of former Church power.

It is very likely that centuries ago the local parson saw himself primarily not as a central figure of local history but merely as the representative of a major state institution: the Church of England. The state Church was led by archbishops and bishops who were national politicians with a seat in the House of Lords; and they were based at palaces located alongside some of the most magnificent buildings the world had ever seen.

An early postcard view of Chester cathedral.

CHAPTER TWO

Cathedrals and the language of gothic architecture

IF THE buildings of the parish provide a glimpse into the daily lives of men and women all over England, the cathedrals offer a magnificent vista of history across centuries of achievement and power. The cathedral is a great place to discover the architectural language of gothic architecture which filtered its way down into thousands of parish churches across England.

LEFT Peterborough cathedral: the fan vault of the retrochoir.

What is a cathedral?

A CATHEDRAL is the chief church of a bishop. It stands in a major city of his diocese, the area under his jurisdiction, and it contains his throne, which is called in Latin a *cathedra* – hence the word 'cathedral'.

It is a general rule with architecture of all kinds that little money can be wasted on unnecessary building work, and so cathedrals were built for specific purposes. On the one hand, they provided a place for Christian worship on a grand scale; but, perhaps more significantly, they also were built for broader political reasons.

At the time when the mediaeval cathedrals were erected, English bishops were men with considerable powers of patronage and with influence in the ecclesiastical courts that determined many aspects of life. They became, and have remained in most cases, members of the national parliament at Westminster. Building a cathedral on a grand scale is a sign both that the Church needed to impress its power on the people, and indeed that it was able to – particularly at a time when civil power was unstable or spending its money on wars and military campaigns. The establishment of the national Church as a centralized, political power in the land was one of the characteristics of Norman and Plantagenet England from 1066 up to the early fifteenth century. It is also true that for a religious establishment to maintain its influence, it must be able to demonstrate not only security, but also the type of unprecedented, awe-inspiring, mystical spaces which could show that the power of the Church was rooted in forces well beyond those that the average citizen came into contact with elsewhere.

Monastery foundations

Some of the best-known cathedrals were also set up as monastic foundations for the Order of St Benedict, with the bishop also nominally the abbot. This meant that the cathedral building itself had to serve a community of monks as well as acting as the principal church in a diocese. There were eight cathedrals of this kind including the vast establishments at Canterbury and Durham, and the building complex naturally encompassed a wide range of accommodation including dormitories and a refectory for the resident community. After the Reformation a similar pattern was adopted

throughout the country: a dean presided over a 'chapter' (or group) of canons. All the cathedrals needed a chapter house as a meeting room for their residents.

The typical features of a cathedral

In spite of the disparity of size, the cathedrals are the place to learn about the type of architecture that you will encounter in so many parish churches. First of all, the layout of even a small church is actually a tiny version of a cathedral; secondly, the cathedrals provide us with many of the finest examples of the styles of architecture and craftsmanship that were copied on a modest scale all over the country.

There is no better place to start an introduction to the English cathedral than Salisbury. This magnificent building, all the more dramatic for its open setting captured by artists such as Constable, was built in only two continuous phases: one which stretched through the middle of the thirteenth century, and another – which saw the completion of the tower and its tall spire of 123 m (404 ft) – in the early fourteenth century.

The fact that Salisbury was built over a comparatively short period of time and the resulting homogeneity of its appearance make it unusual in comparison to the

The interior of Salisbury cathedral, built during the course of the thirteenth century. Its regular, consistent design is unusual for a large mediaeval building.

other well-known cathedrals. But in every other respect it provides a clear and useful guide to the form and purpose of these remarkable buildings.

The construction of Salisbury cathedral was begun in 1220 after its bishop decided to replace a small eleventh-century building, located on an exposed and isolated hill-top, with a new one in a pleasant site in the valley below. The new cathedral was built from east to west. First a chapel dedicated to the Virgin Mary, originally and characteristically called the lady chapel but at Salisbury now named the trinity chapel, was built at the eastern edge of the site. Westwards from here, following an intermediate area, there was a splendid space called a sanctuary built for the high altar; in front of this, still moving westwards, was the presbytery or the area for the priests participating in a service. Adjacent to this was the *cathedra* (bishop's throne). Then came the area known as the choir (or quire), which included the stalls for the cathedral clergy who would themselves have been the singers. North and south extensions, called transepts, were attached either side of this part of the structure.

Some thirty years after the project had started the building began to take on its familiar elongated form. First another, much larger pair of transepts, sometimes called the great transepts, was added west of the choir. The four sturdy columns that defined a central space along the main axis of the building created a crossing. Then came the nave, a vast longitudinal covered area that stretched out westwards from the crossing, flanked the length of its long sides by continuous corridors, defined by columns, called aisles. By the end of the thirteenth century the west front had been completed, together with some attached buildings on the south side: a chapter house for meetings, and a cloister, in imitation of monastery buildings and for contemplation and procession. Finally, following a second phase of construction from 1334, a central tower and spire went up and were completed about 45 years later.

Well before the end of the fourteenth century, therefore, Salisbury had everything that a cathedral required. Although it has now been demolished, it also originally had the stone screen known as a pulpitum that crossed the central part of the building from north to south and separated the clergy in the choir from the public in the nave. Of the features found in these buildings, the only one it never had was a crypt – a basement level chapel, sometimes used for burials.

Cathedrals and the language of gothic architecture

Why a cathedral looks the way it does

EACH PART of Salisbury cathedral, in common with those of all other cathedrals, had an architectural logic of its own which justifies its appearance.

First of all, cathedrals like all churches wherever possible are oriented eastwards for a number of theological reasons. There are references in the New Testament to the significance of the east at the time of Jesus: the apostles turned eastwards at prayer, and the Holy Spirit descended from the east. Jesus was crucified facing west – and therefore to the east of those around him. Furthermore, Jerusalem was for the mediaeval Christian the easternmost city. But making the majority of worshippers in a church building face east was also to make them face the rising sun as the Church day began in the early morning. That meant not only that the sun's light above the head of the officiating priest could daily symbolize the resurrection of Jesus; it also meant that

The plan of Salisbury cathedral showing the principal spaces. The double transepts are an English characteristic.

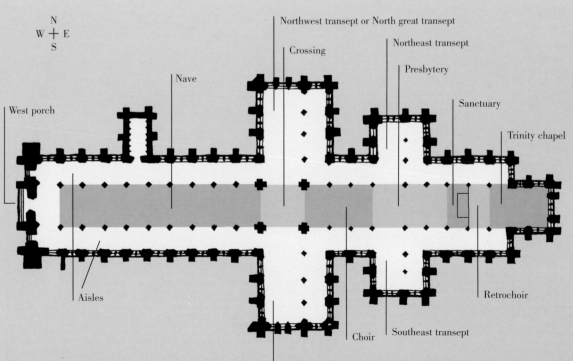

N
W + E
S

West porch

Nave

Crossing

Northwest transept or North great transept

Northeast transept

Presbytery

Sanctuary

Trinity chapel

Aisles

Retrochoir

Choir

Southeast transept

Southwest transept or South great transept

the priest would be lit from behind. As technology allowed larger windows, he might see his congregation relatively clearly, but he was himself obscured by what was sometimes the mystical effect of coloured, filtered light.

So every stage of the cathedral building, from a lady chapel at one end right up to the porch at the other, was arranged so that most people in it would face east and the altars and the celebrants west. That accounts for the long, drawn-out plan of many major cathedrals; it also accounts for the transepts, because each pair provided a further series of east-facing windows.

Southwell Minster: the pulpitum from the quire.

It will be clear from the arrangement at Salisbury that in effect this long building consists not of a single big space but of several self-contained ones. The lady chapel was distinct from the sanctuary and choir. Within the latter, the cathedral chapter faced one another looking north and south, and were therefore distinct from both the west-facing celebrants and the east-facing general congregation. They came in here for the regular services that marked the Church day. On the western side of the pulpitum (the stone screen separating the choir from the nave) and in the large space of the nave the general public could come and go as they pleased. Their purposes might not be particularly religious, because various secular or judicial meetings could be held there. And yet on the other hand until the Reformation they could not escape the purpose of the building because the nave would be filled with minor altars. In some cases altars were set up on the western sides of the broad pillars of the nave. And so yet again the sense of dynamism towards the east was prevalent everywhere one looked.

Roman Catholic cathedrals in England

FROM THE reign of Queen Elizabeth I until 1791 it was illegal for Roman Catholics to worship in public in England outside private or embassy chapels, and it was certainly out of the question for them to build a new church of any kind. From the 1790s onwards, and increasingly following Catholic Emancipation in 1829, many new buildings started to go up – especially in the industrial areas in the Midlands and North West England where large numbers of Irish Catholics were settling. In 1850 Cardinal Nicholas Wiseman announced the establishment of a new hierarchy of Catholic bishops – and that raised the status of the major Catholic churches to that of cathedrals.

The Catholic cathedrals therefore date from the nineteenth and twentieth centuries, and include some very remarkable and unusual structures.

• The principal church of the Roman Catholic Church in Britain is the **Cathedral of the Most Precious Blood**, the seat of the Archbishop

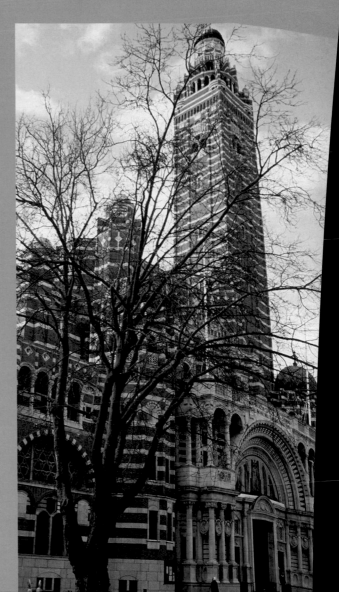

Westminster cathedral in London is the principal church of the Roman Catholic community in Britain. It was consecrated in 1910.

of Westminster. The cathedral was designed by John F. Bentley in 1895 in a powerful Byzantine style which provided a suitable contrast with Westminster Abbey at the other end of Victoria Street and also referred back to the earliest Church structures.

- The earliest cathedral built for the community is also a very important building. **St Chad's, Birmingham,** was designed by the great gothic revival architect Augustus Pugin in 1839 and thus before the re-establishment of the hierarchy. The church had cathedral status because its presiding priest held a nominal, foreign bishopric. Tragically, Pugin's outstanding bishop's house opposite was demolished in the 1960s for a road scheme.

- Pugin also designed the buildings that today function as the Roman Catholic cathedrals of **Newcastle upon Tyne** and **Nottingham.** A further major church by the same architect at **Southwark** was almost entirely destroyed in the Second World War.

- The magnificently brooding Early English-style church of **St John the Baptist** at **Norwich,** designed in 1881 by George Gilbert Scott

junior, was the gift of the fifteenth Duke of Norfolk to the city. The building became a cathedral in 1976.

- In the 1930s Edwin Lutyens designed the vast **Metropolitan Cathedral of Christ the King** for **Liverpool** in a highly personal style which mixed both Bentley's Byzantine with Christopher Wren's baroque. Money (and enthusiasm) ran out before the building rose above crypt level, and on its site a much smaller but undoubtedly memorable and original building by Frederick Gibberd was finally completed in 1967. As with the traditional cathedrals of the past, the building provides a fitting backdrop for a fine collection of works of art by contemporary artists.

- In Clifton, on the edge of central **Bristol,** the Percy Thomas Partnership created the striking **Cathedral of St Peter and St Paul,** designed in 1965 and mainly executed in concrete.

- The classical revival architect Quinlan Terry completed in 1991 the small **Cathedral of St Mary and St Helen** at **Brentwood** in Essex using his own interpretation of the baroque style.

classical architecture in the reign of the seventeenth-century Stuart kings. The earliest buildings were dark and heavy, with low roofs, small windows and very little ornamentation. Once architects had discovered exactly how the load from a heavy roof, tower or walls was transferred down to the ground it became possible as well as desirable to reduce the thickness of masonry down to a minimum. That gave greater scope to the artists and craftsmen on the building site to develop very rich forms of decoration which could carve deeply into the remaining structural stone. As a final stage, the degree of expertise became so finely developed that some major church buildings (for most of the cathedrals had been completed by this time) consisted of little more than ornamental stone skeletons, lit by vast panels of coloured glass. It is this process that created the astonishing sequence of architectural experiments – and achievements – that can be seen in our cathedrals and churches today.

The nave of Winchester cathedral, looking West.

A souvenir from Jerusalem: the Templar church in London

The Temple Church of St Mary, London

VERY FEW buildings have been rebuilt or restored quite as often as this one: its most recent major restoration came after bomb damage during the Second World War. And yet nothing has detracted from the unusual atmosphere and form of this important building.

The oldest part of the church was built by the Knights Templar in the late twelfth century, and it consisted of an arcaded and aisled circular nave – a miniature version of the famous Anastasis Rotunda built around the tomb of Jesus in Jerusalem. It is an early example of Early English architecture, and the combination of the exotic shape of the rotunda with the unfamiliar pointed forms of the new style must have been extraordinary in the London of 800 years ago. There would originally have been a projecting chancel to the East, but this was soon replaced by the large, rectangular chancel where members of the Inner and Middle Temple now sit and which was consecrated in 1240. This is actually an unusual structure too, because it is a hall church: the aisles are as tall as the central space, a feature more common in Germany. The windows, in groups of three lancets, are in the style of the contemporary Salisbury cathedral.

The Temple Church has plenty of remarkable features that have survived all the restorations. Although the nave exterior is mainly Romanesque in style, the interior is distinctly Early English. It seems to have been the first building in London to have used dark, glossy Purbeck marble for its columns, and above the arcade there is a delicate triforium with intersecting arches. Across the floor of the nave you can find thirteenth-century effigies of reclining figures, including at least one Templar knight.

Describing gothic architecture

Architectural historians use a consistent language when writing about the distinguishing features of gothic buildings of all ages. The terms they use are a useful shorthand that will enable you to describe and understand what you see quickly and efficiently, and you will find them time and time again in detailed architectural guides.

The general terminology that is most frequently used is based on the system devised by an architect called Thomas Rickman as far back as 1811. He used four terms to describe the four main styles of gothic architecture which coincide, approximately, with consecutive historical periods. Nowadays we generally use the following version of his system:

- Romanesque, to describe the architecture of the period from Anglo-Saxon times up to the arrival of the pointed arch in the late twelfth century
- Early English, to describe designs from the period from the late twelfth century up to the end of the thirteenth century
- Decorated, to describe designs from a period from the late thirteenth century and up to the late fourteenth century
- Perpendicular, to describe a slightly overlapping period that began in the fourteenth century and continued well beyond the end of the great age of gothic building in the 1500s

You will occasionally encounter an alternative set of terms: 'Norman' for 'Romanesque'; and 'First, Second and Third Pointed' for the other three.

Where to identify the styles

As any description of cathedral architecture makes clear, the different styles of gothic design are most easily recognized from certain distinctive features. These are the ones to look out for:

- The **height** of the major spaces of the building relative to their **width**
- The **shape** of the arches
- The **decorative stonework** in the windows, called the tracery
- The design of the **vault** – the stone ceiling
- The design of the **buttresses** on the outside
- The appearance of the **piers** in the major spaces
- The **delicacy** and **originality** of the decorative carving, for example on the capitals (properly called **impost mouldings**) of the piers
- The horizontal and vertical arrangement of the **internal walls** of the nave and choir.

As time went by, all these design elements showed a tendency towards becoming lighter and more decorative; but remember that different parts of most cathedrals were built or rebuilt at different times, and so you will always need to have a thorough look before coming to any definite conclusions.

Romanesque

'Romanesque' simply means 'the Roman way', and the term suggests, correctly, that building technology scarcely developed in Western Europe between the days of the Roman Empire (which in practice had ended in Britain by the year 410) and the discovery of the pointed gothic arch in the second half of the twelfth century, more than 700 years later.

This did not mean, however, that architecture remained unchanged: Romanesque buildings in Britain are very remarkable structures, often imposing or charmingly decorated in a way that Roman buildings never had been. But it does mean that nothing much had changed in masonry technology. The Romans had been comparatively sophisticated builders compared to the Greeks, and their greatest achievement was the development of the round arch. This was made up from wedge-shaped stones or bricks called voussoirs that maintained a stable shape when arranged in arch form, each voussoir holding the next one in place. Technically, an arch of this kind uses the compressive strength of the masonry in order to span between two columns. Previous civilizations had simply used a straight or flat piece of stone as a lintel, and had therefore

The nave of Durham cathedral. Above the principal arcade there is a tribune and, above that, the clerestory windows.

been limited both by the size of the available stone but also by the fact that they were using the material in tension rather than in compression and thus in opposition to its natural characteristics.

The semicircular arch could be extended continuously in depth to form a barrel-vaulted roof, but it had practical limitations. It required massive stone walls in order to support it, and because it had to form a semicircle in section, it could not rise any higher between two opposite walls than half the span between them. So either the stone vault seemed shallow and weighty, or the supporting walls had to become unfeasibly thick to hold it up.

Nevertheless, some of the greatest achievements of English architecture were built during the Romanesque period in cathedral building, which began before the Norman Conquest in 1066 and ended in the later stages of the reign of King Henry II. Some of the oldest work of this kind, although very heavily restored and altered, can be seen in the nave of St Alban's cathedral, where the white painted walls (and traces of side-altar paintings) create a very different effect from what we have come to expect. The most splendid of all, however, is the cathedral at Durham. This building was started in the years following William the Conqueror's death, and was completed only a few decades later. The powerful nave is enclosed by walls that are separated from the aisles by tall, semicircular arches on sturdy piers, and the stonework is decorated with zig-zags, spirals and other simple geometrical patterns. Above these tall arches is another horizontal row of arched openings, divided into pairs of smaller openings: this opens to a continuous gallery called a tribune. Above these, a row of windows over the aisle roofs, called clerestory windows, let light into the nave from north and south.

Some Romanesque architecture has a more lively decorative character. There are several small churches with very remarkable and animated carvings that have survived to the present day. From the cathedrals of this period, the impost mouldings of the piers in the crypt at Canterbury are very well known: they depict lively scenes with dragons, dogs, goats, and a kind of winged faun playing a stringed instrument.

Much of Norwich cathedral, including most of the lower levels of stonework, is from the Romanesque period, as is the majority of Ely. Externally, Romanesque architecture was solid and severe, its walls decorated with shallow arcade patterns – known as blind arcading where there are no openings behind it – and with flat shallow buttresses known as lesenes.

Cathedrals and the language of gothic architecture

Cathedrals and building materials

CATHEDRALS are also wonderful places to see local building materials exploited to their full potential. Many are built from the varied limestone that stretches diagonally across the country from the south coast around Dorset up to Yorkshire, and these, being generally pale in colour, contrast powerfully with shafts of Purbeck marble.

This contrast is an important feature of the design of Salisbury cathedral, which is built with a fine-grained Chilmark oolite from a quarry nearby in south Wiltshire. Oolitic limestone was used on a further six mediaeval cathedrals. Exeter cathedral was built largely with stone from a quarry owned by the dean and chapter at Beer on the Devon coast. At Canterbury, over to the east, the white stone of Caen in northern France was imported for the great tower as it was for other buildings in the area, but the material has proved susceptible to erosion.

At Durham, sandstone was used. A softer sandstone called New Red was chosen for several cathedrals of the Midlands and North West, and has weathered badly: so much so that in the case of Lichfield much of the visible stonework is actually Victorian. The recent cathedral at Liverpool is faced in the local pink Woolton sandstone; for Coventry, Hollington stone was imported from Staffordshire.

The late Alec Clifton-Taylor, an architectural historian who was an expert on building materials, wrote particularly sensitively on the use of different stone in the cathedrals – buildings he called 'The Master-works of English architecture'.

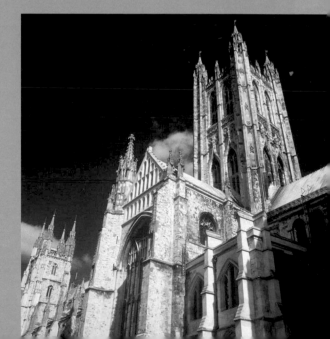

Bell Harry tower over the crossing of Canterbury Cathedral. It was designed by John Wastell around 1496 using a soft white limestone from Caen in Normandy.

The famous
West front at
Wells
cathedral,
Somerset.

Early English

By the time the nave walls at Durham had risen to their full height, masons were on the verge of a discovery. They had decided to span the bays between the huge piers with an X-pattern rather than going straight across in the semicircular barrel_form. Something similar had been done before, for example in the crypt at Canterbury, in the form of a groin vault – a simple intersecting vault with no projecting stone ribs along the junctions. But at Durham they built structural arches to support the vault, and these crossed along the centre line of the nave in a pointed profile allowing tall clerestory windows and giving an airy effect which is somehow quite different from the massiveness of the walls and piers below.

The real breakthrough came only a few years later, and in France. Abbot Suger of St Denis, just north of Paris and now a cathedral, supervised the remodelling of the curved apse that closed the eastern end of his building. He or his masons discovered that if an arch is built in a pointed shape, rather than merely semicircular, the load of the arch itself and any vault it is carrying is directed downwards towards the ground with much greater efficiency. The result is that the arch can go higher, and the piers it is sitting on can become more slender. This was the birth of the gothic style, and it reached England in a few years, not least thanks to the constant traffic of senior churchmen and skilled masons between England and those parts of France ruled by the King of England.

During this first phase of English gothic, cathedral builders were still cautious with their experiments and consequently the overall effect is still of massive walls punctuated by openings. The windows – generally tall and thin – are known as lancets. However the proportions of both windows and arcades had become more sophisticated. Salisbury demonstrates this sense of control perfectly. Every inch of the internal and external walls seems to be part of a neat overall system. The clerestory windows are grouped into triplets, with a tall central lancet flanked by two lower ones. The aisle windows are in pairs; and the transept elevations on the north and south are carefully composed of openings of differing heights and widths. For the first time it seems that architecture might be related to music, dependent on establishing a careful rhythm across different themes. Other cathedrals that are significantly Early English in style include Wells, Lincoln and York, which has a fine set of five tall lancets called the 'Five Sisters' in its north transept. Ripon, which has in fact only had cathedral status since becoming the seat of a bishop in the nineteenth century, has a west elevation entirely made up of lancets.

As would be expected, the Early English style created some distinctive vaulting patterns, the first of the increasingly complex designs that came to characterize the gothic style across the country. Tall piers called responds sprang up from different positions on the walls of the nave, transepts and choir; from these elements ribs began to criss-cross over the ceiling, already turning the pointed arch into a three-dimensional structural form. A bay of the vault that was divided into four, as at Durham and Salisbury, is a quadripartite vault; in parts of Canterbury there are six divisions, forming a sexpartite vault; and at Lincoln and several others there are multiple ribs running from the responds towards the ridge; this is called a tierceron vault.

This first development of English gothic can also be recognized by its distinctive decorative carving. The junctions between the stone ribs that supported the roof were hidden behind bosses, usually carved in leaf patterns. The major piers of the nave were clustered with many more small columns or colonnettes, and the tops of these were increasingly decorated with a pattern called, appropriately, stiff leaf. Small, realistic faces and elegant angels start to appear at the ends of mouldings, or in the spandrels – the approximately triangular spaces between adjoining arches of various kinds.

The magnificent tierceron vault of Exeter cathedral, a masterpiece of the Decorated style of gothic architecture (see page 69), built around the middle of the thirteenth century.

Cathedral fittings

ENGLISH cathedrals contain some surviving mediaeval fittings that have escaped various campaigns to tidy up or modernize their interiors. In particular, a number of cathedrals have remarkable **misericords** – timber ledges on the undersides of hinged seats: when a person was standing up they could perch on it. They are usually found in the stalls of the choir and are carved into fantastical and amusing figures. At Norwich cathedral these include representations of the seven deadly sins, monkeys and dragons; at Gloucester cathedral there are figures of Adam and Eve, Samson and Delilah, and what appear to be a pair of footballers. A particularly beautiful set at Exeter includes an elephant, a mermaid and merman (both elegantly fitted up with fashionable headgear), and a strongman in a loincloth who comically appears to be struggling to support the weight of the person sitting above him. All these carvings date from the twelfth and thirteenth centuries.

The survival of mediaeval joinery is otherwise extremely rare and does not extend much beyond some doors or reused timberwork. In general, anything moveable – or stealable – but too big to place in a cathedral treasury disappeared in one way or another over the years, and fittings such as pulpits were altered as fashions changed. At Peterborough cathedral, however, there is a rare mediaeval brass lectern in the traditional form of an eagle.

On the other hand, cathedral libraries contain many treasures. That at Hereford includes the thirteenth-century **Mappa Mundi**, or map of the world; and the collection of St Paul's cathedral in London includes **Wren's Great Model** (see page 81).

Many misericords have delightful ornamental carvings. These Victorian ones include tiny frogs (right).

Decorated

The Decorated style, which coincided roughly with the reign of kings Edward I, II and III, was in fact more varied in its appearance than the other three major categories, and architectural historians from Victorian times onwards have enjoyed dividing and subdividing it up into sub-categories, each with its own distinctive and complicated terminology. But the basic characteristics of Decorated architecture are clear. Windows became wider, and were embellished by increasingly complex tracery of different types. The structural system behind the pointed arch became more sophisticated, essentially starting to turn into a true three-dimensional system. Flying buttresses that projected from outside walls directed the load of the vault away from the face of the building; finials, little towers or pyramids of stone, helped divert the thrust downwards. The result was that external walls could be made thinner still, and could be pierced by larger openings. And the walls between the main structural openings and elements began to disappear as decoration began to flow across the various surfaces.

The nave of Exeter cathedral, which was built across the middle of the fourteenth century, is a fine example of the Decorated style. Instead of sturdy piers

Flying buttresses form part of a sophisticated structural system that relieves the church walls of part of the downward thrust from the stone vault.

surrounded by colonnettes there are whole sheaves of tiny columns, their impost
mouldings delicately flowing into one another. Above them the respond shafts terminate in what look like bunches of flowers. Over the nave arches there is a lacy blank
arcade called a triforium, and above that an ethereal series of clerestory windows. The
vault itself is a particularly spectacular example of the tierceron type with a row of
prominent bosses. Large decorative carved panels elsewhere in the cathedral, for
example the row of fourteen angels under their niches on the minstrels' gallery, are
integrated elegantly into the architectural conception as a whole. At Lincoln cathedral
the 'Angel Choir' is studded with delicate ornamentation of all kinds, in the spandrels
and up and down the shafts of the highly ornamental, deep tribune (gallery) openings.

Among the most beautiful examples of Decorated carving are the famous 'Leaves of Southwell' in the chapter house of Southwell Minster, a small and mainly Early English building. The 'leaves' are realistic vines, ivy, hops and many other leaves and flowers carved into the impost mouldings of the niches around the edges of the hexagonal room as well as into the capital of the column at the entrance.

As the fourteenth century progressed, masons experimented further with different patterns of tracery for the ever-widening windows. At first this took the form of a flat panel of stone, pierced with simple geometrical shapes: this is called plate tracery. In time, this panel became lighter and more delicately carved, and the geometrical patterns in it came to be more decorative. This type is called geometrical tracery. Elsewhere, the curving upper parts of the mullions (vertical bars across a window) and transoms (horizontal bars) formed patterns that resemble weaving; this is intersecting tracery. Woven shapes and geometrical patterns began to intersect, creating little swirling shapes called daggers or mouchettes: this is called curvilinear (or, sometimes, flamboyant) tracery. Or, alternatively, they created an even, net-like pattern over the whole of the top of the window known as reticulated tracery.

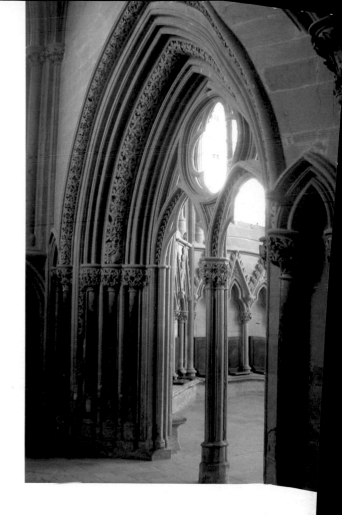

A glimpse into the chapter house at Southwell Minster, home of the famous leaves.

Perpendicular

As the centuries passed, English gothic architecture became less and less like the continental version, so that by the end of the Decorated phase the patterns being created in tracery and carving bore little resemblance to the generally more fanciful shapes seen in the same period in France. The Perpendicular stage completed this process, and there was not really any equivalent phase abroad.

A magnificent church from the golden age of gothic architecture

St Mary, Ottery St Mary, Devon

THE PARISH church at Ottery St Mary is so impressive in scale and construction that it could almost be a cathedral in miniature. In fact one of its most unusual features, the pair of transept towers, appears elsewhere only at Exeter cathedral. Built as a collegiate church for a community of 40, this building is a wonderful example of mid-fourteenth-century architecture at its most impressive: indeed, a visit to Ottery St Mary reinforces the sense of amazement that structures like this were conceived as centrepieces for the tiny and shambolic villages of the period.

In spite of its period, this church is not a typical example of Decorated gothic: its windows do not have the flowing, ornamental tracery associated with it. At Ottery St Mary it is the richness of the walls and vaults that is so striking. The vault itself varies throughout the building; in the nave the most interesting features are perhaps the bosses. In the chancel the design is highly decorative, with a flowing, floral theme. Monuments include the beautiful fourteenth-century tombs of Sir Otho and Lady Grandison, members of a well-connected political family. It is important not to miss the sixteenth-century Dorset aisle on the north side: built originally for local parishioners who were not members of the college, it has a splendidly elegant Perpendicular vault that is reminiscent of wafting palm fronds — the swan song of gothic architecture before the Reformation.

From 1849 the great Victorian architect William Butterfield began a lengthy restoration of this church and the unusual monumental font is an excellent example of his distinctive style.

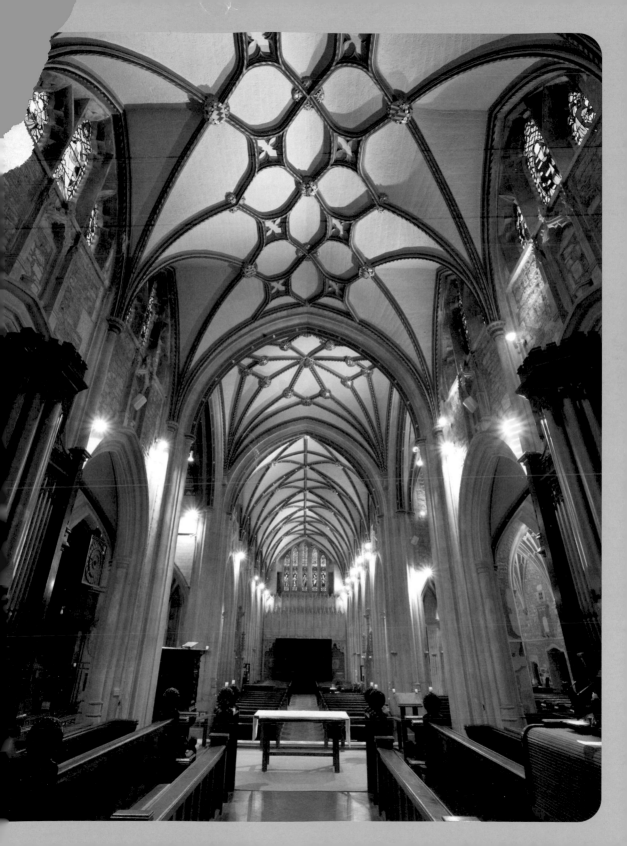

The distinguishing feature of the Perpendicular style was the changed relationship of wall to window. A large church was no longer a masonry box with windows cut out: it was a series of windows held together by a masonry frame, although that frame could well be a highly ornamental one. Of all the cathedrals, only Bath and Oxford have any substantial Perpendicular work in them. The greatest examples of the style are the chapel of King's College, Cambridge (built over the course of nearly 70 years, from the mid-fifteenth to the early sixteenth centuries), and the chapel built to commemorate King Henry VII at Westminster Abbey. The abbey, incidentally, became a cathedral for ten years after the Reformation, but was eventually redesignated a Royal Peculiar: a church under the control of a dean, and ultimately of the monarch, rather than a bishop.

A Perpendicular gothic window is broad, topped with a shallow pointed arch. Tracery is predominantly vertical.

These remarkable buildings have another distinguishing feature: the fan vault. We have seen how the structure of a roof became increasingly busy, as more and more ribs were added to create amazing decorative effects. Tierceron vaults became star vaults, with intermediate ribs known as liernes forming intricate patterns. The final stage of their development was for the ribs to merge with the stonework infill so that the structure eventually became a shell, a series of structurally homogenous interlocking half-cones with convex sides and a decorative thickening that appeared to be (but generally was not) the last remnant of a visible structural grid. The cloister at Gloucester cathedral has a particularly fine fan vault. In the choir of Oxford cathedral, which also functions as a college chapel, the fan vault has extraordinary pendant

bosses that seem to be defying gravity; they are in fact the lower parts of voussoirs (wedge-shaped stones forming part of an arch or vault) that have been greatly extended downwards but at their upper level form part of largely hidden constructional arches.

While the Perpendicular style came too late to be a major feature of cathedral architecture, you will encounter it many times in some of the largest and richest parish churches – particular in the East Anglian woollen towns that reached the peak of their prosperity towards the very end of the mediaeval period.

The chapel of King's College, Cambridge, is the outstanding masterpiece of the Perpendicular gothic style. Its breathtaking fan vault was complete by 1515.

Another well-known fan vault can be found at King Henry VII's chapel at Westminster Abbey. These ceilings are among England's greatest structural achievements.

The characteristic features of English cathedrals

GOTHIC architecture flourished all across Europe, and every country has its own examples of breathtaking structure and artistry. English gothic however developed several distinct features of its own which are unusual or even quite absent from continental examples:

Very large East windows, such as this famous one at Gloucester cathedral, are a characteristic of the English gothic style.

- **A flat east end** with a great east window. Many major French churches have apses, or rounded east ends, sometimes with chapels located between flying buttresses, radiating around a curved ambulatory. This in fact was the situation at St Denis where the gothic style first developed, but also in some of the earliest surviving churches and Norman-era cathedrals in England. Later on, though, a rounded apse was used only as conscious imitation of French work. Westminster Abbey, built by Henry III who was steeped in French culture, is an example of a French-style building with an apse.
- **Transepts**. Continental cathedrals do have transepts, but in England they are more prominent and there are more of them. In some cases there are several sets the length of the church. The retrochoir, for example, can be developed in the form of a transept as it is at Durham, Wells and Hereford. A pair of minor transepts, as at Salisbury, is quite common. Some cathedrals, including Peterborough

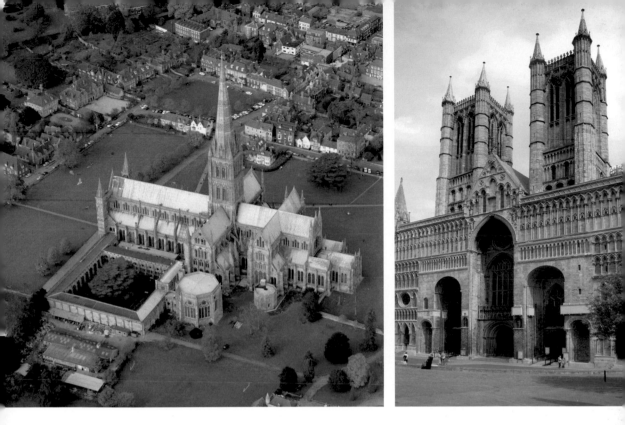

and Lincoln, have what is in effect a further set of transepts at the far western end of the nave.

- **A central tower.** It is possible that part of the role of the great transepts in English cathedrals was to help support a major landmark at the centre of the building. The tower at Canterbury, called 'Bell Harry' (see page 65), is a particularly fine example in the Perpendicular style, with beautiful vaulting that can be seen from the crossing below. Continental cathedrals more generally have towers at the west end and a slender timber construction (called a flèche) over the crossing.

- **A screen-like west front** and **small western porches.** Wells, Lincoln, Lichfield, Peterborough and Salisbury have broad, predominantly rectangular western fronts that screen the end of the cathedral and provide a magnificent backdrop to groups of statues. Porches in continental cathedrals tend to be much more substantial than in England: in all of these four examples, the western doors are surprisingly modest. Some of the details of English cathedrals are also unique to this country:

- Shafts of **Purbeck stone.** This dark shiny stone, a Jurassic limestone which resembles (and is often called) marble, was popular as a material for slender colonnettes

The characteristic features of English cathedrals

around openings. It generally contrasts sharply with the stone used for the rest of the building.

- Upper windows in the form of a **triangle with convex sides**. Lichfield cathedral has these, and so does Westminster Abbey.
- The ancillary buildings of an English cathedral have their characteristics, too. The **polygonal chapter house** is an English feature; they generally have eight sides, but that at Lincoln has ten. And the **cathedral close**, which separates the great church from the rest of the town, is also English. Most continental great churches are surrounded by houses.

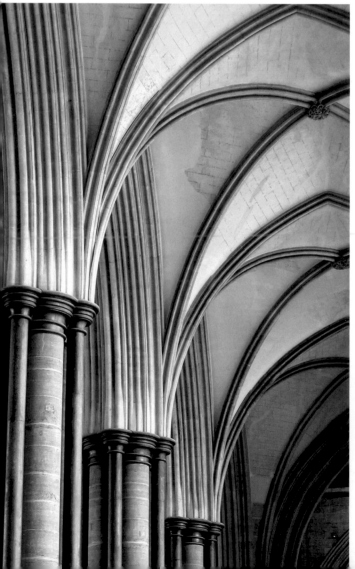

LEFT
At Salisbury cathedral some of the column shafts are made from a dark limestone called Purbeck marble which contrasts attractively with paler stones.

BELOW
A chapter house with a polygonal plan is a characteristic feature of an English cathedral. This one at Lincoln has ten sides.

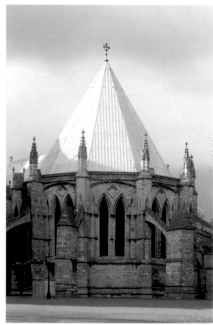

The major French cathedrals

THE MAJOR cathedrals of France deserve a full study of their own for the richness of their architecture and craftsmanship. In general, they differ from English ones in their taller, narrower proportions, their multiple aisles, and the spire-like flèche that stands instead of a tower over the crossing. The eastern end of French cathedrals is usually in the form of a curved apse that incorporates a series of chapels between highly ornamental flying buttresses. In fact several French designers also worked on English buildings: William of Sens, from a town on a tributary of the Seine south of Paris, designed the rebuilding of the choir of Canterbury Cathedral in the 1170s. One of the masons working on Westminster Abbey was probably also a Frenchman.

Nevertheless, French cathedrals are quite distinct in their style and arrangement:

• **St Denis**, where the rebuilding of the apse resulted in the birth of the gothic style, is also remarkable for its twelfth-century western front. This is a neatly composed arrangement of blind and glazed lancets, on the one hand still massive and yet on the other a step towards a sophisticated gothic elevation. The central part of the church between the apse and western end was rebuilt in the thirteenth century, and it contains the tombs of the French kings and queens.

• **Laon** cathedral, north-east of Paris, is best known for its lively pair of towers at its western end, where charming statues of farm animals look down from a great height over the three massive entrance porches.

• **Nôtre Dame** cathedral in **Paris**, which like several major French churches was in fact very substantially restored in the nineteenth century, has what might be called a classic French arrangement: the nave and choir with their double aisles are really a continuous volume, barely interrupted by the transepts which do not project beyond them. The western end of the cathedral has a pair of towers either side of a bold, wheel-like rose window; the eastern end is a semicircular apse, with vast flying buttresses.

- **Chartres** cathedral, where French kings were crowned, was rebuilt after a fire from the end of the twelfth century. The eastern end of the church is both wider and longer than the nave.
- There are splendid cathedrals of a similar date at **Bourges**, **Le Mans**, **Amiens** and **Reims**. With continuous interior views from their west porches looking beyond the nave and to the apse at the far side, and with often breathtakingly high arcades and narrow vaults, these buildings generally have more of a mystical and dynamic quality than their English counterparts.
- At **Beauvais** the mediaeval masons planned the tallest vault of all: 48 m (157 ft). Unfortunately it collapsed, and today's cathedral consists only of a truncated east end.
- The **Sainte-Chapelle**, the royal chapel in **Paris** close to Nôtre Dame, is by any standards one of the most remarkable gothic buildings of all. The upper chapel is a single small space but with a soaring vault; its walls have been reduced to a skeletal minimum and are richly glazed from top to bottom. It is often compared to a jewel box.

Nôtre Dame cathedral in Paris, which was heavily restored in the nineteenth century, is one of the symbols of Paris.

St Paul's cathedral, London

THE WORLD-FAMOUS cathedral of England's capital city is, perhaps ironically, in quite a different style than any of the famous mediaeval ones that in so many ways symbolize the country and its culture. Until the Great Fire of 1666, Old St Paul's (as the mediaeval building is now known) was also a gothic cathedral – in fact, one of the most impressive and with a splendid central tower. The cathedral was destroyed, along with 87 parish churches and seven-eighths of the entire built area of the City, in the blaze, which was not finally extinguished for several days.

By the time the Fire broke out, Christopher Wren, an astronomer from Oxford University who had Church connections, was already employed by the dean and chapter to investigate repairs and improvements to the old building. After the calamity, their first hope was to restore it as it had been. But it eventually became clear that this was unfeasible. Wren had recently been experimenting with architectural designs for new buildings in both Oxford and Cambridge, and his first hope was that the new St Paul's would be a splendid classical church on a centralized plan: something in the manner of St Peter's in Rome, but designed in one go as a geometrically-perfect building rather than the result of more than a hundred years of additions and alterations. But his Great Model scheme of 1673 was rejected by the Church, who thought it too continental – which meant too Roman Catholic at a sensitive time in British Church politics – and he was asked to go back and come up with a design that would include a nave and transepts and would thus more closely resemble English tradition.

The result was what was called the warrant scheme of 1675. This looked something like a hybrid between a gothic plan and classical decoration, and as the project proceeded Wren was able to

The West front of St Paul's cathedral, London. Although highly unusual for an English cathedral, this building has come to symbolize the capital.

The interior of St Paul's cathedral. The stone vault is supported by flying buttresses but these are hidden externally by a tall screen wall.

make it appear more coherent. In fact the great triumph of the eventual building is the clever way in which he created a structure which did indeed combine the old and the new.

With its broad, colonnaded portico (porch) at the western end and its tall dome rising above the crossing, St Paul's cathedral looks at first like a pure classical building. But in fact all the major structural elements owe a great deal to the English gothic tradition. The western front is really a modern version of the traditional screen, and behind it there is a pair of western transepts. The great vaults of the cathedral are supported by flying buttresses, as indeed they have to be if they are not to collapse; these are hidden by screen walls that run around the outside edges of the building. And the dome is itself an umbrella-like structure in timber and lead which hides a brick cone that rises from the crossing to support the hefty lantern and cupola (small dome) 111 m (365 ft) above street level.

None of this is to belittle Wren's achievement. He was a masterful sculptor of space, and created a magnificent backdrop for major public events. The fact that he was so inventive with the detailing of the building – he designed the western towers when he was nearly 80 – is all the more remarkable considering that he never saw the baroque architecture of Italy at first hand. The Anglican Church of the period was a different type of body from the one that had built the gothic cathedrals: it was a more overtly political and civic organization, and it was in parts aggressively anti-Roman Catholic. At all events, the building of St Paul's and of the new City churches was to have considerable influence on architects across the country.

Cathedrals and the language of gothic architecture

Anglican cathedrals since Wren

THE EIGHTEENTH century was a quiet time in the history of the Church of England, but the religious revivals of the Victorian era resulted in a period of church building unequalled since mediaeval days. New dioceses were established throughout the country, and with the new bishops came new cathedrals. At first large parish churches were promoted in status, but from the late nineteenth century onwards several new buildings were erected, usually following prestigious competitions that attracted the best of the architectural profession.

• The cathedral at **Truro**, designed in 1880, was the first new one to be founded in England since Salisbury over 650 years previously. The architect was John Loughborough Pearson, one of the most accomplished late gothic revival architects, who used here an Early English style. The building incorporates the mediaeval church of St Mary,

Giles Gilbert Scott was just 22 years old when he won the competition to design Liverpool's Anglican cathedral. The building took 75 years to complete.

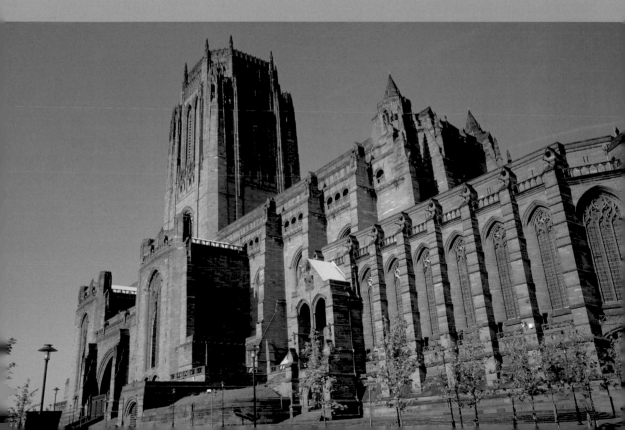

which has become an aisle chapel to the south of the choir.

- In 1903 Giles Gilbert Scott, a very young Roman Catholic architect and the grandson of the gothic revivalist George Gilbert Scott, won the competition for the design of the new Anglican cathedral in **Liverpool**. Plans for the building were revised considerably during the long period of its construction, which did not end until 1978, 18 years after the architect's death. As executed, the building owes a great deal to English traditions: it has a pair of great transepts and a massive central tower, and the whole is designed in a free version of late gothic. On the other hand, it is idiosyncratic: nearly symmetrical along both axes, it has a vast central space below the tower. It is undoubtedly as powerful an addition to the city's skyline as the mediaeval cathedrals were to their own towns in their day.

- Edward Maufe designed a new cathedral at **Guildford** in 1932. Building work was greatly delayed by the Second World War, and the cathedral was not consecrated until 1961. Designed in an austere modern interpretation of gothic, the contrast between the warm reddish-brown brick of the exterior and the creamy stone and whitewashed interior is particularly effective.

- At **Coventry** the cathedral, an impressive parish church that had been elevated to cathedral status in 1918, was almost entirely destroyed in an air raid of November 1940. The new building, designed by Basil Spence, was opened in 1962. An airy and evocative structure filled with the work of the best artists of the post-War period, Coventry cathedral is in many ways a close descendant of the mediaeval cathedrals.

Coventry cathedral was designed by Basil Spence, the winner of a prestigious competition in 1951. It contains many artworks by leading artists of the day.

The relevance of cathedral design

THE GREAT cathedrals of England are clearly very different from the average parish church. Very few parish churches, for example, have stone-vaulted roofs, and it was the desire to build these ever more dramatically that accounted for the experimentation with structure and style that characterizes the different periods of building.

Nevertheless, getting to know cathedral architecture is always a first step in understanding the village church. First of all, the arrangements of many of the internal spaces of small churches are closely related to those in the cathedral: the overall logic is the same. Secondly, we will encounter everywhere gothic design in carving, metalwork and glass that is derived from the most splendid and complete examples found in cathedral architecture. And finally the cathedrals can demonstrate on a grand scale many other decorative and instructive features which are reproduced in miniature throughout the country. Although both the Reformation and the Civil War wrought terrible damage on the interior of the cathedrals, in some cases because of an earnest desire to rid them of idolatrous images but in others because of gratuitous vandalism, we can still find traces of grand iconographic schemes which were copied on a small scale wherever people could afford to do so. The western screen fronts at Wells, Lincoln and elsewhere were filled with statues of Church fathers or saints, and their windows were often part of a complex overall plan of biblical stories and didactic images that taught churchgoers about the history of their Church and its lessons. And we will encounter these things on a tiny scale wherever we go throughout the country.

The West front of Wells cathedral provided the splendid setting for an array of religious statues illustrating lessons in theology for the onlooker.

CHAPTER THREE

Discovering the parish church

NOW THAT you are familiar with the layout and style of a great gothic cathedral you can easily appreciate the logic behind the appearance of a small parish church. It is time to take a tour around one of these buildings and to identify its characteristic features.

LEFT A view into the chancel of the twelfth-century church at Studland, Dorset.

Approaching the church

THE SETTING of every church in its location is different. Nevertheless, mediaeval builders were generally consistent in the way in which they positioned a new church on its site, and so the chances are that you will enter it in much the same fashion wherever it is and wherever you are coming from.

A mediaeval church would originally have been located in a churchyard, and most village ones are still like this. That means that you can see at least half of the outside of the building as you come up to it, and so you will be able to grasp its basic layout almost immediately. Like cathedrals, mediaeval churches are nearly always built so that the congregation faces east. You will find that in many cases the path through the churchyard leads you up to a porch and main entrance located towards the western end of the south side of the building. Occasionally the porch is on the opposite side of the building: at the western end of the north side. Either way, you will most likely arrive at a position where the length of the nave stretches away from you once you are inside, and you can get a good sense of the scale of the building as you enter it.

Town churches were, increasingly, built on more restricted sites. Although they tried to avoid it, Victorian builders sometimes had no choice as to the orientation of the building because they needed the main axis from the porch to the altar to be as long as possible. In these situations, it often happened that the church was built with its nave running perpendicular to the street. This provided the second common type of approach: one where the entrance is at the western end, under a large west window.

Liturgical geography

Because churches were nearly always built so that the congregation faced east, people have tended to refer to the area around the altar as being the 'east' even when, in a few cases, the church's orientation does not in fact follow the standard. This has given rise to an alternative set of compass points called liturgical ones, according to which the altar end is always said to be at the 'east' and the other cardinal points are rearranged accordingly.

The easiest way to make it clear that you are referring to these liturgical directions rather than real geographical ones is to use capital initial letters, and that is what this book will do. In this way, an altar which is in fact at the north end of, for example, a town church is said to be at the 'East' according to its liturgical geography; its street porch, which is really at the south, is called the 'Western' porch. These terms may seem at first confusing, but once you are used to them you will find the system convenient – and nearly all guide books use it.

It is just as well that church builders made every effort to ensure their building faced the traditional way. The famous church of St Paul in Covent Garden, London (see page 148), was planned to face west so that its entrance portico at the eastern end would form an impressive feature for the piazza in front of it. At the last minute before its opening, the local bishop ordered the orientation inside to be reversed so that the altar would be at the eastern end after all. The result was rather a clumsy elevation and people now had to filter in along the sides to get in. But, conveniently, the proper orientation was restored: the 'East' end of the church really is in the east.

A church nave looking towards the chancel from the West end.

One of the great wool churches of East Anglia

Holy Trinity, Long Melford, Suffolk

THE SPLENDID East Anglian churches of the Perpendicular era form one of the greatest architectural treasures in Britain: built as painful civil and foreign wars were finally coming to an end in the late fifteenth century, they are perhaps a symbol of a stable and peaceful nation about to take its place on the international stage. With their vast light-filled naves they provide quite a different type of experience from the intense sculpted spaces of earlier gothic architecture. Although Lavenham is more dramatic and March in Cambridgeshire has the best array of timber angels, Long Melford must surely be the stateliest of them all.

It is certainly one of the longer churches, with an interior dimension of 47 m (153 ft). The broad windows with their slender mullions almost fill the walls both at arcade level and up in the clerestory, so the whole pale grey nave is ablaze with light. The lady chapel is remarkable: it is surrounded on all four sides by an ambulatory. The tower's exterior facing, incidentally, is comparatively modern: it was completed in 1903 to designs by G.F. Bodley, one of the most sensitive of all gothic revival architects.

The church has excellent examples of interesting details. One of the windows depicts three hares sharing three ears between them, creating a symbol of the Trinity. One of the most popular sights in this building is another window that has the portrait of Elizabeth Talbot, Duchess of Norfolk, which is thought to have inspired Tenniel's illustrations of the Duchess in Alice in Wonderland. There is also a squint (see page 114); and the tomb of wealthy local clothier and benefactor John Clopton, in the wall of its own chantry to the north of the chancel, also functioned as an Easter sepulchre (see page 98). In the ornate chantry there is a rare and evocative stained-glass depiction of a crucifix of lilies.

A first look at the building

THERE ARE many features of the exterior of a church – not least, the porch itself – that are important parts of its layout and which give a valuable guide to its construction date and style. But it is perhaps more useful at first to step inside and look into the nave.

At once it will be clear that even the smallest church is a version in miniature of a great cathedral. Only a small number of churches, largely built since the middle of the twentieth century, have attempted anything else. You will find yourself towards the Western end of the nave, with the seats inside facing East. At the Eastern end you will see an altar. The altar will very probably be set some distance in front of the Eastern wall, and there will be seats around it that are arranged differently from the others.

This is where you can make your first assessment of the space that you find yourself in. At once you will be able to distinguish:

The layout of a typical church, showing the important elements.

- The **nave**. This is the main space facing the altar where most of the congregation will sit.
- The chancel. This will be a distinct space Eastwards of the nave.
- The **altar** may be in the chancel, or it may stand immediately in front of it.

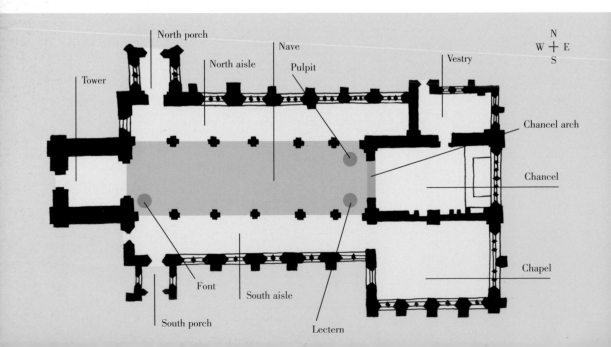

North porch

Nave

North aisle

Pulpit

Vestry

N
W ✛ E
S

Tower

Chancel arch

Chancel

Chapel

Font

South aisle

South porch

Lectern

- The **aisles**. These are spaces that run the length of the nave, at either side of it and separated by an arcade. Some churches have no aisles; others have one or both.
- The **transepts**. These are rare in a parish church, but some have them – particularly if the building was more important in pre-Reformation times.

Once you have appreciated these major spaces you can then go on to make out the other common features of the church:

- The font. This is most likely to be at the Western end of the church.
- A chancel screen that divides the nave from the chancel – if there is one.
- A pulpit for a preacher to give a sermon, usually located in front and to the left of the altar.
- A lectern, a reading desk traditionally in the form of a brass eagle, for readings from a bible during the course of church services.
- A set of **organ pipes**, often at the West end of a church, or on the North side near the chancel.
- The **windows**. The East window of a church is likely to be the largest one, although sometimes the West one can be impressive too.

Although there are many variations in all of these features in the thousands of churches around the country, their general pattern is usually surprisingly similar. You will find most of them in churches of all denominations, and wherever you are, you will discover that it is their particular combination of proportion and style that gives a place its own atmosphere and architectural character. If you look out for them as soon as you enter you will soon get a sense of what the church is like; and if you can describe them accurately you will easily convey your impressions to others.

Tall transepts lead North and South from the crossing to the West of the chancel of this church.

Looking carefully around a church

ONCE THE overall form of the place has become clear it is time to discover how exactly a church is designed, and to learn how to appreciate its unique qualities. The place to start is the chancel, which will be the area most carefully laid out, and where the position and arrangement of what you find there is most significant.

A chancel is an architecturally distinct area that is a small-scale equivalent of a cathedral sanctuary.

The chancel and the communion table

Look Eastwards from the nave in nearly every church and you will at once see the chancel, the distinct part of the building that does the job of the cathedral choir,

presbytery and sanctuary in miniature. It is often separated from the nave by an opening called a chancel arch.

Of course a parish church does not need to seat large numbers of clergy as a cathedral would; so this area was traditionally reserved for the choir and the celebrant – that is, the person officiating at the service who is probably, but not necessarily, the incumbent.

The chancel or the Eastern end of the building will always be the focal point of the church even if it is not a distinct space, and usually it is still dominated by an altar. You may find that an altar in general use has been placed in the nave, but often an older one has remained in its original place as well. The correct name for an altar in a Protestant church is a communion table, and that is the name that will be used henceforth in this book. The significance of this name is that, as in the first Christian churches, it is simply a table made of wood, and its purpose is for placing the communion bread and wine on display before the celebrants. During services there may also be an altar cross and candlesticks on the table.

Reformation churchmen wanted to abolish stone altars because they seemed to them to be too reminiscent of physical sacrifice rather than of a shared rite. As a result, they are very rare in the Church of England and if you can identify one, it will probably have been placed or replaced there in recent times. Stone altars are usually marked with five incised crosses on the top.

You will find that the communion table sits on a predella, a platform, at the Eastern end of the chancel. The table will have a coloured frontal for most of the year (see page 115).

The chancel arch viewed from the nave.

There are a number of other features that you may see in the immediate area of the communion table:

A reredos (pictured overleaf) is an ornamental panel placed against the wall behind the communion table, which can rise as high – or higher than – the bottom of the East window. Sometimes the reredos sits on a ledge which is also called a predella. The reredos can be painted or carved; pre-Reformation and Roman Catholic ones may have statues; Anglican ones more probably have texts or symbols. An altarpiece, such as one of the familiar Flemish ones, could either form part of the reredos or sit independently at the back of the communion table. The frame or the overall setting for a reredos is called the retable.

Some communion tables, particularly early twentieth-century ones, are located under a canopy which is called a ciborium because it was intended to resemble a

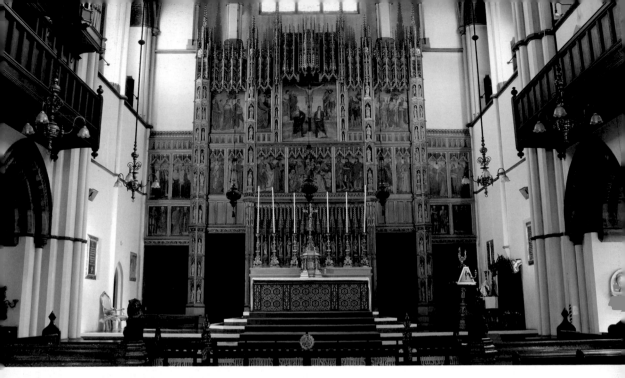

A reredos. This one, constructed in the 1870s, fills much of the East wall of the chancel.

ciborium in its other meaning: a cup or bowl for communion bread. A permanent canopy on columns is called a **baldachino**, a word derived from the Old Italian word for 'Baghdad', the name and place of origin of a kind of cloth. The special vocabulary used when describing the architectural features of churches is a reminder that these things were once regularly discussed by churchmen using the mediaeval languages of Europe, including Latin.

There are a few other features that recur in chancels:

- The **sedilia**: if you stand with your back to the communion table and look to your left you might find a row of three or four built-in seats on the South side for the celebrant and his assisting deacon and subdeacon. These seats are sometimes stepped, following the predella. A single seat is called a sedile; a group is called a **prismatory** (pictured on page 98). A prismatory may include:

- A **piscina**: a stone basin for rinsing hands and the communion plate. There may be a fixed shelf nearby called a **credence table**. A canopied niche built into the wall for these is called a fenestella.

- Opposite the piscina, there may be an **aumbry**: a built-in store for the vessels used for the communion; nowadays it is also used for sacraments reserved or left over after a communion service (see page 100).

Discovering the parish church

How to date a church

IT IS NOT always easy to work out the age of a parish church, because the building may well have grown over a lengthy period of time. It might also have been restored, and today, as in the nineteenth century, restoration work is so thoroughly carried out that it is difficult to see the join. Very crisp stonework and sharp, distinct details are unlikely to be more than 100 years old, whatever the age of the original fabric underneath. Furthermore, old memorials could have been moved from an earlier location, for example when part (or all) of an older building was demolished. Even where the church walls seem to be mediaeval, the roof may be Victorian. In a sense, therefore, it is often the style of the church and its character that are more important to establish than an actual period of construction.

Nevertheless, there are some ways in which it is possible to get a sense of the building's general period of construction. Try first of all to break down the overall shape into its constituent parts such as nave, chancel and aisles. Then see whether those parts share a common design vocabulary. The windows are a good place to start. Are all the aisle windows the same? Do they appear more modern than those in the clerestory, or upper part of the nave? If you can establish that a particular type of window seems prevalent and original across the building, you may be able to categorize it as 'Early English', 'Decorated' or 'Perpendicular' (see pages 62–75), and thus get a sense of the period of the main part of the construction.

Detail of an impost moulding from a blocked archway in the North wall of the choir of the priory church at Finchdale, Durham.

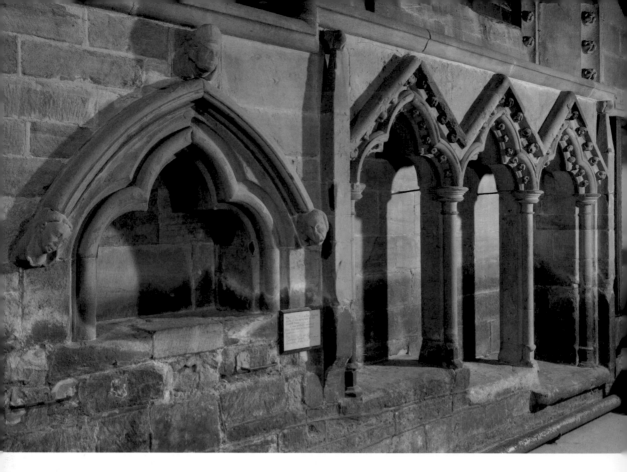

A prismatory, consisting of a row of three sedilia (right) and a piscina (left).

- An Easter sepulchre (pictured on page 159), may also be found on the North wall of the chancel, facing the sedilia. This is a feature of a mediaeval church that rarely survived the Reformation. It is a symbolic representation of Jesus' tomb that was used for special ceremonies between Good Friday and Easter.
- The communion rail, the original function of which was to protect the communion table. They were mainly introduced in the seventeenth century, and acted as a kind of substitute for a demolished chancel screen (see opposite).
- There may be stalls for the **choir** facing each other at the Western end of the chancel. Do not be surprised if there is also a drum kit or an electronic keyboard!
- The organ console and pipes, and the door to the **vestry**, may also be in, or near, the chancel – usually on the North side.
- There may be screens to the North and South of the chancel to separate it from side chapels. These are called parclose screens.

Discovering the parish church

In some cases a chancel was added to a church after the nave was built; sometimes, the nave was added to a chancel which had formerly been a tiny chapel.

Upkeep and refurbishment of the chancel were, until comparatively recently, the personal responsibility of the incumbent.

The chancel screen

In mediaeval times there was nearly always a screen between the chancel and the nave, and if it has survived or been rebuilt it will be an important feature of a church. Originally its purpose was similar to that of the stone pulpitum of the cathedral that separated the clergy in the sanctuary from the congregation in the nave; at parish level it allowed secular events to take place in the church without encroaching on the chancel area.

Many chancel screens, which are sometimes called choir screens, have a character that is as distinctly English as that of the typical church itself. They are usually made of timber and take the form of a frame filled with decorative panels; there will be an opening in the centre, and often an ornamental top. Some screens from the mid-nineteenth century onwards are made of wrought iron.

A simple timber chancel screen, converted in Victorian times from a mediaeval rood screen.

The services of the Church of England

ONE OF THE main aims of the founders of the Church of England was to simplify the complex traditions of worship that had grown up in the Roman Catholic Church. The Book of Common Prayer, which was first published in 1549, provided the approved liturgy for use in all English churches and also stated the formulas for all daily services and for a limited number of special occasions. The Book of Common Prayer was revised on several occasions, and it is the version of 1662, with minor amendments, that is in use today. It includes a lengthy introduction which explains its intentions and

A communion chalice holds the consecrated wine.

applications, and its use is supported by law. The General Synod, the internal parliament of the Church of England, authorized in 2000 an alternative service book called Common Worship.

The daily rituals prescribed by the Book of Common Prayer include morning and evening prayer, usually known in the Church of England as matins and evensong. The most important service in regular worship is, however, holy communion, which in the Protestant Church is a symbolic recreation of Jesus' last supper with his disciples. The celebrant consecrates wine and bread, which represent Jesus' blood and body, and administers them to the congregation; the exact purpose and significance of these consecrated elements, as they are known, has always been a major matter of debate between Christian denominations. Holy communion is alternatively known as the eucharist, and in the Roman Catholic Church is called the mass.

The Book of Common Prayer also includes services for baptism, holy matrimony, confirmation and funerals.

The screen is sometimes called a rood screen because before the Reformation it may have been combined with a carved depiction of Jesus' crucifixion called a rood. This feature is often fixed to a beam, called a rood beam, which ran above or along the top of the screen. Protestant reformers disapproved of this combination because of the inclusion of religious images, and many roods were destroyed; in some cases, the screen itself was cut down to form a low balustrade. Rood screens were, however, revived from Victorian times onwards.

A rood, supported by a rood beam.

Above the screen there may have been a rood loft, a platform for singers or musicians, reached by a rood stair – which, if it was built into the masonry of the church, may have survived longer than the screen itself.

A pair of Essex churches dedicated to St Mary, at Stebbing and Great Bardfield, have remarkable stone rood screens.

Perpendicular splendour in a merchant city

St Mary Redcliffe, Bristol

THIS IS A church with large transepts that is as impressive as a cathedral, and some of its features are as unusual as any that can be found in a much larger building. Bristol was a leading international port in the late Middle Ages and its merchants were travelling across the globe. Perhaps it was they who brought back the inspiration for the exotic ornament found in this church.

The most surprising element of St Mary Redcliffe is the first part of it the visitor encounters: the north porch. It is hexagonal in plan, which is in itself remarkable; but the decoration that covers its surface is almost fantastical. The doorway is surrounded by floriated cusps and ogees – S-shaped mouldings – that are Persian, North African, or possibly even Indian in appearance. The rest of the decoration, which climbs almost all the way up the windows, is a lively forest of crockets and niches. The porch's interior is as splendid as a miniature chapter house. In the nave your attention will be drawn immediately to the soaring ornamental vault, studded by countless carved bosses and seemingly only scarcely supported by masonry. Its many ribs give it a lacy quality. Some of the tracery is unusual, too: in the West and East windows of the south transept a broad fringe of quatrefoils sails around the central three lights. The large number of ornamental bosses high up on the vaults is remarkable: there are said to be well over 1,000 of them, some of them delicate, original and comic. One is carved with a rare circular labyrinth pattern.

Queen Elizabeth I visited the church in 1574 and she is said to have declared that it was 'the fairest, goodliest, and most famous parish church in England'.

The nave

The painted
wagon roof of
this church
soars high
above the nave.

The nave forms the body of the church and is the place where the congregation sits.
You may find as you first look into it that a communion table has been placed at its
Eastern end. This is in fact a very ancient tradition which is being increasingly
revived: modern churches are usually built in this way from the start, and it is more
likely than not that an old
church will have been
altered. The usual term for
this type of table and the
area around it is a worship
space. This arrangement
allows the celebrant and a
small congregation to
engage more closely with
one another during
services.

The nave is the part of
the church that most closely
resembles the equivalent
part of a cathedral. There
may be an arcade, clerestory
windows and even (in the
grandest buildings) a triforium – just as you have seen
them in the previous chapter
(see page 70), but on a
smaller scale. So a nave can
be characterized in a similar
way: by the number of bays
(that is, the vertical division
into arched or windowed
openings), and by their
style, using the categories
you learnt in Chapter Two
(see pages 62–75).

A ch
of the

...ch nave is unlikely to have a stone vault although there are some in the [...] country that were at their most prosperous during the later Middle Ages, and few more that were built during the gothic revival period. In any case, it is always rewarding to look up and see what form the ceiling takes:

- A hammerbeam roof. Only the grandest timber roofs take this form: there are spectacular ones in the great Perpendicular-style churches of East Anglia. A hammerbeam roof is one in which the roof structure is supported on large brackets which project from the wall. These brackets support **hammer posts** – upright timbers that form part of the framing of the roof.

    The splendid appearance of a hammerbeam roof is due to the rich and substantial mouldings of the brackets, which are sometimes ornamented with carved figures.

- A barrel roof has a curved or semicircular section, and is panelled on the inside to make a continuous timber vault.

- A wagon roof is similar to a barrel roof, but with a polygonal section. One sometimes sees the structure for roofs of these kinds that never had the intended ceiling attached to it.

- A tie-beam roof is any kind of timber structure, broadly triangular in section, that has a series of horizontal beams holding it together. Variations of these are common in churches: some have king posts rising up vertically from a tie beam to the underside of the ridge (the topmost longitudinal member); some have queen posts – smaller paired vertical posts.

- Many nave roofs simply have **trussed rafters**: that is, the angled rafters that run from the ridge down to the wall plate at the top of the wall are held together by a collar that runs horizontally between them, or by braces that run at an angle – or both.

    You will find instances where the architect designed walls and piers to support a stone vault that was never eventually built.

Aisles

Unlike a cathedral with its need for side chapels and through-routes for pilgrims, a parish church need not necessarily have aisles. The modest timber roofs of small churches do not require the complex structural system that supports a stone vault, and therefore there is no technical reason to have them either.

You will, however, encounter aisles that were built for a variety of reasons. In the case of Victorian and early twentieth-century churches, church builders believed that the

Looking from
the nave
towards the
South aisle in a
typical church.

double-aisled, cathedral-type layout was architecturally the most satisfactory and complete way of organizing a church, and so they constructed them for that reason. But historically aisles were added to the North or South side of a church either because a benefactor had endowed a side chapel, or because during a period of prosperity a congregation grew and needed more space. Adding an aisle to a church required altering the windows on the nave walls, possibly by adding a clerestory and nearly always by creating a new arcade. There are some examples of churches where an existing church became the aisle of a new one, and the two sit side by side, sometimes uncomfortably. In all these cases you can look out for windows and decorative details that changed over time, thus allowing you to identify which part of the building was built at which period.

Discovering the parish church

Seating

The first word that comes to mind when thinking of sitting down in a church is 'pew'. But in fact that is misleading on two counts. The first is that the long timber seats immediately associated with churches and generally called pews should really be called benches. And the second, as you will soon discover, is that many churches have disposed of their benches altogether and replaced them by seating which they consider to be more flexible.

A pew in the true meaning of the word is a raised, enclosed seat that was rented by an individual or a family, who paid pew rents towards the maintenance of the church. These paid-for pews were sometimes surprisingly large: there are some which had curtains, several seats and even a private stove for heating, not unlike a box at a theatre. Non-paying members of the congregation sat or stood wherever they could find a space, usually at the back or sides of the church.

Victorian benches replaced private pews in most churches during the nineteenth century.

Pews survived everywhere until the nineteenth century. Then church reformers became anxious to facilitate churchgoing among people who did not otherwise attend, and began to insist that church attendance was both rent-free and also relatively non-hierarchical. Pews were swept away and replaced by the long benches that have become so familiar. Although most of these were standard types that were made and sold in bulk by church furnishers, some have unusual and decorative features such as carved panels or flower-like timber finials at their ends. Many of these have now been replaced by flexible seating that allows the church to be used for informal meetings.

It is possible to find surviving pews today. They are generally smaller than the largest type, but can be ornate with doors and other fittings. Alongside the well-known castle at Stokesay in Shropshire there is a manorial parish church that was, unusually, rebuilt during the Commonwealth (1649–60), and here you can find a set of pews in an interior that has survived without significant alteration.

The gallery

In the early nineteenth century a great deal of government money was spent on providing churches for newly developed residential areas in industrial towns. At this stage the priority was to have as many seats as possible for the congregation, and so experiments were made in the basic form of the church in order to increase their capacity cheaply.

The result was the development of an idea which had already been tried in the early eighteenth century: an upstairs gallery where large numbers of people could sit overlooking the service below.

Galleries were usually placed at the West end of the nave, but often over the aisles as well. This was logical from a planning point of view but could be awkward visually, because the nave windows to the North and South were cut in two or truncated horizontally. This can be seen in many of the cheap churches built in the early nineteenth century by the Church Commissioners (see opposite).

A galleried arrangement suited many Protestant denominations, but were disliked by nineteenth-century Church of England reformers because they considered them unhistorical. In some places, galleries were taken out; new ones have been very rare in Anglican churches since the mid-nineteenth century.

The nave will also contain three major fixtures: the pulpit, the lectern and the font.

Families of churches

AFTER MEDIAEVAL TIMES churches were no longer built continuously across England: there were bursts of activity during specific periods. The result is that you can very often guess the approximate construction date of a particular post-Reformation church.

Very few churches were constructed during the uneasy times of the early Stuart era and the Commonwealth. After the Great Fire of London in 1666, however, the first of a series of distinct families of church began to go up:

• The **Wren churches** in the City of London. Over 50 churches in the City are attributed to Christopher Wren, but he himself did not design all of them: he had a number of talented assistants, including Nicholas Hawksmoor who later became famous in his own right. Architecturally, however, the churches have a great deal in common with each other. Many of the surviving ones have attractive and unusual spires – the first attempt to combine the classical language with a recognizably English form.

It is important to note that most of the original Wren churches were

badly damaged in the Second World War, and those that were not demolished afterwards were altered internally during restoration.

• The **baroque London churches**. An act of parliament, usually called the 50 New Churches Act, was passed in 1711 to pay for new churches around the edges of London that would match the recent Wren ones. Only a few were actually built, but among the ones that were constructed are some remarkable buildings, including several by Hawksmoor, James Gibbs and Thomas Archer. Many have imposing porticoes and grand flights of steps.

• The **commissioners' churches**. Because parish boundaries were mediaeval and centred around the old villages, there was a serious shortage of churches in the residential centres that grew up with the Industrial Revolution; furthermore, almost no churches were built at all during the latter part of the eighteenth century. In 1818, three years after the battle of Waterloo, an act of parliament was passed which established a board of commissioners to fund new churches for these areas, not least with an eye towards keeping the working population under the influence of the Church's teachings.

Many hundreds of these buildings were erected, even if not quite the 600 intended, and subsequent acts of parliament continued the project. The churches were mainly very cheap in construction, consisting of a single rectangular room with minimal decoration. They usually had galleries as a way of increasing the number of seats. Their style was either nominally neo-classical or gothic, although a few talented architects managed to make some visual impact. The well-known architect John Soane designed some of these in an idiosyncratic neo-classical style; Charles Barry, the architect of the Houses of Parliament, produced some gothic ones early in his career.

- **The gothic revival.** It was the gothic revival, which mainly ran from the 1840s up to the end of the nineteenth century, that re-established the mediaeval-type church and which resulted in the appearance of most churches you will see today.

- **Modernist** churches. Several leading mid-twentieth-century architects were attracted to the idea of a building as a kind of sculpture, and the design of a church with its symbolic functions and large open spaces provided an effective opportunity for some highly experimental ideas.

The pulpit

The pulpit is the place where the celebrant or a visiting preacher delivers the sermon, an address to the congregation on a religious theme. The pulpit therefore was always located in the nave rather than in the chancel.

Pulpits were usually positioned to the North-West of the chancel arch. Some mediaeval pulpits have survived: they were made of timber, usually oak, or stone, and consisted of a raised, enclosed platform supported by a central post: the effect is often likened to a wine glass on a stem. The panels of the external faces of the pulpit were sometimes ornamented with biblical scenes or sculpted figures (see Chapter Five). A canopy called a sounding board or tester was placed over the pulpit so that the preacher could be better heard.

After the Reformation, when a chancel screen might have been removed or reduced and when a church service was intended to express a common fellowship rather than a mystical event, a sermon was increasingly a central feature of church life and consequently the pulpit became a more significant part of its furnishings. The design of post-Reformation pulpits expressed their new importance, and old engravings show that in the eighteenth century they were placed not to one side but right in the centre of the Eastern end of the nave, dominating

A timber pulpit in a typical mediaeval church.

even the communion table. Occasionally the pulpit was actually moved Westwards towards the centre of the nave. These pulpits could have two or sometimes even three decks: the preacher stood at the top; the lesson from a bible was read from a desk in the middle; and the parish clerk – whose role was more significant than before or since – would sit at the bottom. A flight of curved or spiral stairs with an ornate balustrade, such as the one that survives at St Martin-in-the-Fields' church in Trafalgar Square, London, provided the preacher with an impressive route to the top.

A brass lectern. The eagle represents St John the Evangelist.

These double- or triple-decker pulpits were disliked by nineteenth-century church reformers from the growing Oxford Movement (see page 168) because they were associated with a period in the Church's history when mediaeval traditions had been suppressed and when sermons had replaced liturgy and ceremonial at the heart of a religious service. The result was that they were disposed of, or physically cut down: you may find one that shows signs of having been taller. The reformers also revived pulpits that were more mediaeval in design, and they restored the mediaeval practice of having a separate and distinct place for the reading of the lesson: the lectern.

The lectern

The lectern is a reading desk located opposite the pulpit, on the other side of the chancel arch, at the East end of the nave. Traditionally it has taken the form of a brass eagle that supports a bible on its back: this is a model taken from surviving mediaeval examples. Other lectern types include revolving timber ones with places for two or even four books, or hinged ones attached to the chancel screen or a wall.

The font

The third of the three major freestanding objects generally to be found in a nave is the font, traditionally located at the Western end of the church. The font is a basin which is filled with water that is used in the ceremony of baptism, or admission to the Church. On this occasion the celebrant will bless the new member of the church congregation – generally still a baby – by touching them with water from the font.

The font is usually positioned near the entrance to the nave, and this has always suggested a symbolic link between coming into the building and entering the Church as a new member. Very old fonts have survived, including some from the Anglo-Saxon era.

Side chapels

One of the characteristics of pre-Reformation worship was the way in which it was diversified throughout the Church rather than being concentrated around a common eucharist with a single preacher. As you

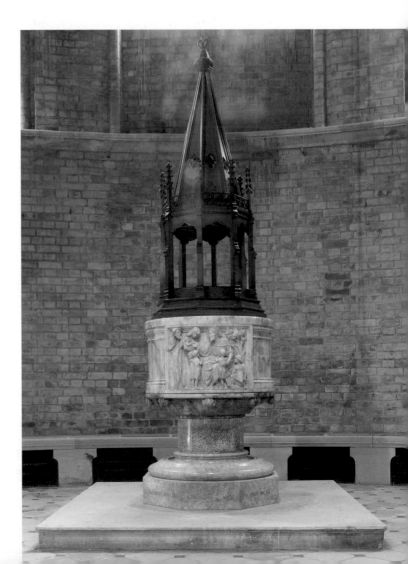

A carved stone font with a timber font cover.

A side chapel. This is a lady chapel, to the South of a chancel.

have seen in Chapter Two, cathedrals were once filled with a large number of subsidiary altars at which prayers were offered for the intercession of saints for particular people or events. Chief among these various minor spaces was a lady chapel, because of the important place that the cult of Mary, the mother of Jesus, held in Western Christianity.

The larger parish churches were built with lady chapels too. Likewise, the pious would endow other chapels where prayers could be offered in perpetuity for their salvation: chapels of this kind, which would include both an altar and a tomb, were called chantry chapels. In some places, major landowners built and furnished chapels of considerable size for this purpose. Elsewhere, religious or professional groups of various kinds built chapels for their members. In many medium-sized churches you can find a chapel that approximates in size to the chancel located to the North or South of it. Sometimes you will find there a squint or hagioscope – a hole cut through a chapel wall so that the priest in the chapel could follow the service at the high altar.

The Church's colours

WHEN VISITING a church you will find that the predominant colour of clergy vestments and furnishings such as the communion table frontals varies according to the church season. In Advent and Lent the colour will generally be purple; at Easter and Christmas it will be white or gold; for much of the rest of the year, for example during the long period of Ordinary Time over the summer, it will be green.

Each of these colours has its own significance which is much older than the rituals used in today's churches. The colour green has always been associated with growth and renewal; white signifies purity, and gold represents preciousness and grandeur. Purple is on the one hand the colour of royalty and so its use at Advent implies the coming of the king of heaven; it is also, however, a symbol of penitence, and for that reason it is used at Lent. Because the colour red is associated with fire, it is used at the festival of Pentecost to represent the flames of fire that, according to the Acts of the Apostles in the New Testament, rested that day on the heads of Jesus' apostles.

Certain celebrations have traditional colours associated with them: white for weddings and baptisms, and purple for funerals. There are other events which will change the appearance of the inside of a church: on or near Harvest Sunday, near to the autumn equinox in September or early October, you may find arrays of fruit and agricultural produce. This is in fact a ceremony of heathen origin which only found its way into the Church in the nineteenth century. Sometimes you find corn dollies, plaited from sheaves of corn, which still have a somewhat pagan appearance.

On Palm Sunday, which is the Sunday before Easter, the liturgical colour is red, and the congregation is given crosses made from dried palm leaves. On Good Friday and until Easter morning, the communion table will be left uncovered.

The Roman Catholic Church has its own instructions and traditions for use of liturgical colours, and images of saints may be covered during the fortnight before Easter.

Colour plays a further part in the life of the church when used in the depiction of certain figures and scenes, especially in the Roman Catholic and Eastern Churches. Here the most commonly seen colour is a shade of pale blue, associated with Mary, the mother of Jesus, who is usually seen wearing a robe of this colour. According to Roman Catholic tradition Mary was 'assumed' – that is, miraculously transported – into the heavens at the end of her life instead of dying. This shade of blue is therefore a further reminder of her celestial nature and role, in the eyes of some, as Queen of Heaven.

Mary sometimes wears her blue robe together with a garment of red, which, because it is the colour of blood, is associated with sacrifice. Grey is used for repentance – it reminds the onlooker of the 'sackcloth and ashes' with which the prophet Daniel turned in penitence to God.

Artists throughout the centuries have exploited the association of colours with particular figures. An important character at the centre of a crowded scene could be easily identified by an onlooker if they wore a robe of a certain colour: Judas Iscariot is sometimes seen wearing yellow, a colour as much linked with cowardice or treachery as with heavenly radiance. Perhaps more significantly, though, artists evidently recognized that it was through the masterful and persuasive use of colour as a whole that believers could be captivated by a religious painting.

Images of Mary, the mother of Jesus, often inspire devotion in Roman Catholic churches.

116

The religious leaders of the Reformation disapproved of the idea that a person's soul might be saved by virtue of their having provided in advance of their death a fund for their salvation on the day of judgment. The chantries were closed down and the monarch confiscated their endowment. Nevertheless, the rooms or buildings created for them usually remained. In today's church you will find that they have been converted into chapels for occasional use, or for celebrating communion when the congregation is small. Some chapels have been built or furnished as war memorial chapels, or in commemoration of particular events or people.

The porch

Now that you have become familiar with the important features of the typical church, it is time to turn back and have a further look at the route by which you entered.

The porch of a church is more than just an entrance lobby: various church rituals and customs were enacted there. The major theme that links these is the idea of the porch as the way in not just to the physical part of the church but also as symbolic of an entrance to spiritual purity. The service of baptism traditionally began there, as did several customs connected with marriage. The banns – the announcement of an intended wedding – were proclaimed in the church porch in mediaeval times by the priest, and the marriage service itself could commence there. A ceremony called the 'churching of women' held in the porch marked the return of a woman to membership of the congregation after child-birth. In perhaps a similar but reverse fashion, a funeral service would pause there before continuing outwards to the churchyard. For all these reasons a porch might be an impressive part of the building, in architectural terms a satis-fying visual termination to the South-Western end of the church in counterbal-ance to the usually more ornate Eastern end. Before the Reformation a porch might be furnished with a holy water stoup so that those entering the building could anoint themselves as a symbolic way of purifying their hearts. The stone benches that sometimes can be seen in porches would have been useful on a number of different occasions.

Porches evidently fulfilled other functions too – in particular, ones where an activity needed to be carried out under shelter but in public. There are cases where a porch is known to have provided someone with shelter, or even was used to lock them up temporarily. In some rare but usually very attractive cases the porch had more than one storey, and upper rooms were employed for conducting business or for the residential use of a priest: at Cirencester parish church in Gloucestershire there is a spectacular three-storey porch that originally functioned as the town hall, and there is a similar one not far away at Burford in Oxfordshire. Parish notices were published in the porch, as they still are.

A church's main porch is traditionally found on the South side of the building.

Discovering the parish church

The exterior of the church

NOW THAT you have become familiar with the major elements of the interior of the church, it is time to leave through the porch to have a closer look at the outside of the building.

In mediaeval or mediaeval-style churches the external appearance will closely reflect the functions and the structure of the interior. What makes these buildings so special is the way in which their designers managed to bring together all the various elements to create a building with a satisfying overall shape. One of the most important elements in creating that successful overall form is the tower.

In addition to this important architectural role, a church tower has at least two other and related functions: it signals the church from afar, and it provides a place for the bells to hang so that they can be rung loudly and clearly. This latter function was so important to the mediaeval church that even churches without a tower generally have a small structure on the roof at the Western end of the nave, called a bell-cote, in which to place them.

Mediaeval bells were used to summon the congregation to prayer at regular intervals in the days before clocks or watches, and many of them still survive. It is also important to remember that until the invention of the railway timetable there was no need for clocks across the country to be coordinated with each other, so the ringing of these bells was for most people an important fixture of daily life. In time the practice of ringing a number of different sized bells in sequences was established, a tradition known as change-ringing.

A church tower was almost certainly the tallest masonry structure in the mediaeval village, and consequently it could be used as a lookout or a beacon. Many have clocks or sundials on them.

Tower design

Although the layout of a church followed a certain pattern, the design of the tower will vary greatly from place to place. In some cases this is because local building materials influenced its form: flint, brick and stone have very different properties which will limit the use of some design features and encourage others, especially when

Church towers vary in style and splendour across England depending on local wealth and building materials. This needle spire is at Snettisham in Norfolk.

constructing a tall, slender building. But it is also because the tower can exhibit a range of characteristics that are special to it and not necessarily related to its structural stability or any function that might go on inside.

The design of a tower can be classified in a number of ways:

- Its **horizontal section** – that is, its shape on the ground. Nearly all towers are rectangular or square in plan, although there are a number of round ones built from flint, mainly in East Anglia. It is also worth noticing, however, that the shape of a tower can change subtly as it works its way up.

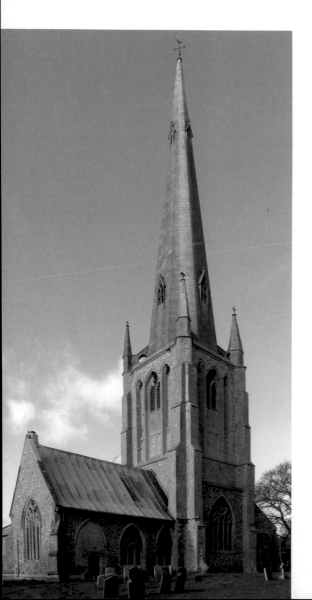

- Its **location** in relation to the rest of the church. You discovered in Chapter Two that a central tower, placed over the crossing between the nave and transepts, is a traditionally English arrangement, and some of the larger churches imitate this. A very small number of church towers are actually freestanding. Usually, however, the tower is placed at the Western end of the church, and often at the South-Western or South-Eastern corner.

- The **stages** of the tower. A stage is the term for the horizontal division of the tower – what in a house would simply be called a 'storey'. Seeing how the designer of the tower designed stages that slowly evolve or balance each other is one of the great pleasures of looking at churches.

- The **spire**. A spire is by no means a purely English feature, for some of the most dramatic and impressive ones can be found in Europe, especially in the west of Germany. But the range of spire types and the prevalence of the spire as a feature of the village church are characteristic of England. A tower and spire together are called a steeple.

Church architects

SOME ARCHITECTS are best remembered for their church designs. The Scots baroque architect James Gibbs, although a Roman Catholic, designed several churches including one which has become an internationally recognized landmark: St Martin-in-the-Fields in Trafalgar Square. It was this building which first superimposed a spire over a portico to create the distinctly Anglican type of classical architecture that spread widely through the Episcopal Church to New England.

There are whole families of architects whose reputation rests largely on their designs for churches. This is perhaps most true of the many members of the Scott family. George Gilbert Scott, who was born in 1811, was the most prolific architect of the nineteenth century and designed many important public buildings, including the front of St Pancras station and what is today the Foreign and Commonwealth Office in London. He designed a large number of churches in a convincingly mediaeval gothic style, from small village ones to impressive buildings such as those at Doncaster, Halifax and Kensington; large college chapels in Oxford and

Cambridge; and cathedrals in Edinburgh and Newfoundland. He also restored many mediaeval English cathedrals.

Scott's son, also George Gilbert Scott, was a Roman Catholic, which in England limited his career as a church builder. He designed the Catholic cathedral in Norwich, as well

Sir George Gilbert Scott, architect of the Albert Memorial and the Midland Grand Hotel at St Pancras, was a highly accomplished and prolific church architect.

as a number of significant smaller buildings. His brother John Oldrid Scott, also a church architect, designed the remarkable Byzantine-style Greek Orthodox cathedral in Bayswater, London.

George Gilbert Scott junior had two architect sons who were also important as church designers: Giles Gilbert Scott and Adrian Gilbert Scott. Giles Gilbert Scott designed the Anglican cathedral in Liverpool as a young man, and built several small Roman Catholic churches around the country, as well as one further cathedral (at Oban in Scotland); like his grandfather, he also designed several school and college chapels.

The various members of the Pugin family were also best known for their church designs – in this case, almost exclusively for the Roman Catholic Church. Augustus Welby Pugin designed from the 1830s onwards the first authentically mediaeval-looking churches. He also planned the large and splendid buildings which are today the Catholic cathedrals of Birmingham, Nottingham and Newcastle upon Tyne. His eldest son Edward Welby Pugin designed several churches in an ornate French style, and Edward's brother Peter Paul Pugin ran a large architectural practice specializing in churches and church institutions.

Ninian Comper (1864–1960) was an architect admired entirely for his church design work, which consisted of a few new buildings, such as the dramatic St Mary's, Wellingborough, but primarily of many church fittings all over the country.

It is not unusual for an architect to make their reputation as a result of their design for a prestigious church. This was the case not only with Scott at Liverpool but also with Basil Spence in Coventry after the Second World War. The partnership of Maguire and Murray achieved fame after they designed an influential centralized church at Bow Common in London in 1956 (see page 214).

Augustus Welby Pugin provided the inspiration and the talent to transform Victorian architecture.

Spires are usually timber constructions covered with lead, slates or tiles, although some are made of stone. The basic type of a spire is defined by the way in which it rises up from the tower. Spires tend to be octagonal in plan whereas towers are usually square, so there will need to be an arrangement whereby the octagon evolves out of it. The resulting form is usually a broach spire — that is, the spire rises from a set of four pyramid-like forms at the corners of the top of the tower.

Other spire forms include a crown spire, where the whole of the construction takes the form of a series of open buttresses; and a needle spire, which is one that simply rises from within a parapet on top of the tower. You will find variations all over the country. You will also see towers that terminate with lanterns — cages of open stone or timber work — or with unusual gables, such as the saddleback towers that have tall pitched roofs.

English church spires have many varied forms. Their height often balances the length of the nave to create a satisfying composition.

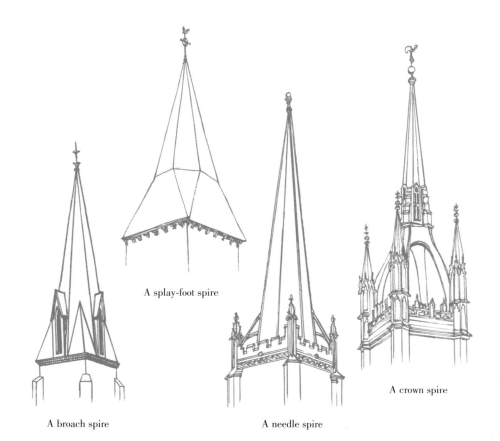

A splay-foot spire

A broach spire

A needle spire

A crown spire

The neo-classical church

YOU HAVE seen how St Paul's cathedral in London is different in its style from the great majority of English cathedrals. Similarly, the number of English neo-classical churches is small compared to the many thousands of mediaeval or gothic revival churches, but at least some of these buildings are distinctive and influential.

The principal difference between the English neo-classical church and the traditional one is that the former are generally designed around a single space. Sir Christopher Wren was not allowed to create a centralized plan for his new cathedral, but in the case of his designs for small parish churches the practical difference between what he wanted and what tradition demanded was not so great. Since the Reformation, worship in an English church had been concentrated around the preacher and so there was little need for separate chapels or a chancel screen. Wren therefore designed a series of churches in London which brought all the available space together into a unified form.

Wren was not the first designer of neo-classical churches in England: that was Inigo Jones, in the early seventeenth century, during the reign of James I. Jones' churches, however, had copied the longitudinal form of the traditional church, as indeed some Italian renaissance designers had done. But Wren was influenced by recent international developments and in particular by the baroque churches of the Italian architect Giovanni Bernini. Bernini designed buildings that seemed like huge sculptures, and which experimented with dramatic effects of light and shade.

Most of Wren's churches in the City of London had to be built comparatively cheaply, and they all had to allow the usual internal East-West seating arrangements, with the communion table at one end and the font at the other. But the surrounding space could be made to flow continuously around the worshippers in a way that recalled Bernini's work. At St Stephen Walbrook, by the Mansion House in London, Wren designed a central dome that seems to hover above the nave and which powerfully conflicts with the traditional plan of the building below (see page 160). St Mary Abchurch is a tiny building, almost square in plan, and like St Stephen it has an impressive dome. St Benet Fink, which was destroyed in the Second World War, had a ten-sided nave with an oval dome at the centre. St Swithin, also gone, was square in plan but with an internal colonnade that created an octagon at its centre.

Discovering the parish church

The architecture of neo-classical churches

NEO-CLASSICAL is the style of all architecture which from the fifteenth century onwards has imitated or has been based on the principles of surviving ancient Greek and Roman buildings. Its revival first occurred during the period known as the renaissance, a time of increased interest in the classical world and of rapid development in the arts and literature which flourished in the cities of today's Italy.

The principles behind the design of ancient Roman buildings had been described in a surviving text of the first century AD by an architect named Vitruvius. He described what was expected of a professional architect, and also gave details of the plans, proportions and specific elements used in the design of public buildings.

Both ancient classical architecture and the revived version of it,

A Corinthian capital in a neo-classical church.

eventually named neo-classical, were highly disciplined in their use and development of these proportions and details. The result, following the renaissance, was a type of building entirely different from that of the mediaeval gothic churches. Neo-classical buildings were symmetrical, and used repetitive units such as rows of columns and windows in ordered lines across the whole of a facade. This contrasts strongly with the gothic church that expresses externally the changing functions of the interior, and which can change in style from one end to another.

The central feature of all classical architecture is its use of the orders. Each of these is a different stylistic language which is applied to the various parts of the building in imitation of examples found on ancient Greek and Roman temples. The columns and the decorative detailing at their capitals (heads) or bases will generally indicate which order has been used:

- The **Doric order** has sturdy columns with vertical channels called flutes cut all around it. A Doric column sits directly onto a platform with no decorative base. Its capital usually resembles a simple cushion of stone.

- The **Ionic order** has slender and smooth columns, and sits on an ornamental base. It has a distinctive capital in the form of volutes – possibly representative of rams' horns and sometimes likened to the handset of an old-fashioned telephone.

- The **Corinthian order**, which is similar in its proportions to the Ionic one, has a capital that resembles a carved sheaf of acanthus leaves.

These three orders were derived from Greek architecture, which started to take on a stylized form around the fifth century BC. Imperial Roman architecture developed them, and also contributed further orders of its own. The entablature, or stone band around the tops of columns that includes a cornice and frieze, also varies in style according to the order it is associated with.

Renaissance and later neo-classical architects had to be very inventive in order to adapt ancient architecture for modern use; they were inspired as much by triumphal arches and other secular buildings as by the ruins of temples. One of the pleasures of looking at neo-classical churches is discovering how their architects created original compositions through the use of ancient forms and by bending the rules of design.

Neo-classical churches were built right up to the gothic revival of the 1840s, and then, after an interval, reappeared towards the end of the nineteenth century. These later ones were mainly built with Wren's designs in mind, though their simple longitudinal plans are closer to the earliest Christian basilicas in Rome than they are to Wren's extraordinary experiments.

St John's church in Lambeth, London: a Doric commissioners' church of 1823–4.

Variations between churches

THE FEATURES that you have found in the typical parish church are those that you can encounter almost everywhere. You will nevertheless find distinct differences between the furnishings and fittings in the churches you will visit. Some of these are variations between Anglican churches of different types, and some are between the Anglican churches and those of other denominations.

The Church of England

Surprisingly perhaps, you will find greater variety between different Anglican churches than you will between the Western Christian denominations. This is because since the early nineteenth century the Church of England has represented a wide range of religious attitudes between the evangelical wing on the one hand and the Anglo-Catholic wing on the other. Parishes and their parochial church councils tend to belong to a particular stream of Anglicanism, and consequently the incumbent appointed is likely to maintain the atmosphere that the congregation expect or want. The term 'broad church' derives from a description of a congregation or Church leadership that aims to be as accepting as possible of the different Anglican groups.

An evangelical church will be focused on the preacher. That means that the church is likely to be a single space, and the seats may be arranged as if in an auditorium or even a theatre in the round. You will find many churches that have been refurbished in order to do this, and it is usually for this reason that communion tables have been brought forward towards the congregation from their traditional place at the Eastern end of the chancel.

Many evangelical churches make a great feature of the rite of baptism, so you may find that the font is mobile or has been moved Eastwards towards the communion table. These buildings avoid visual distractions, so the building may be painted white and have little ornament. Evangelical movements in general encourage social activity outside the church and you are likely to find evidence of this in the form of notice boards or posters for activities and reports. The presence of modern musical instruments is generally also an indication of an evangelical church.

By contrast, the Anglo-Catholic wing of the Church of England grew up in the mid-nineteenth century as an attempt to revive the style and liturgy of the English

Discovering the parish church

Church before the Reformation. Their churches therefore are much more decorative, and have retained or brought in traditional fitments like chancel screens or even roods. Anglo-Catholic worshippers continue to revive traditions such as processions from one part of the church to the other on special occasions, and that means that the separation of the building into distinct areas is more important to them than to evangelicals. These areas may include features that are in general rare in the Anglican Church: a blessed sacrament chapel for the reserved consecrated bread and wine, or spaces where confession can take place.

Roman Catholic churches

The architecture and furnishing of a Roman Catholic church, built since Catholic worship became legal in the late eighteenth century, will not differ greatly from that of an Anglo-Catholic church: the significant fact is that most Catholic churches will as a matter of course have all the features that only some Anglican ones have. These

Evangelical churches place great emphasis on participation, and traditional fittings can be replaced by a stage and auditorium. Music and singing are often an important feature of worship.

will include separate chapels dedicated to specific saints, although in a Catholic church worshippers will direct their prayers directly at the saint concerned. As a result, you may find shrines or images of saints in greater abundance, and almost certainly at a greater intensity. One of the few distinct features of a Catholic church will be the confessional – a cubicle for a private conversation between a priest and a parishioner.

The revived Roman Catholic Church of the nineteenth century could have reintroduced chantry chapels, a tradition forbidden to Anglicans since the Reformation. In practice, only a handful of these were built and even they are not all truly chantries in the proper sense of the word since priests were rarely endowed to maintain them.

Roman Catholic churches throughout the world were reordered – that is, rearranged – from the 1960s onwards in order to meet the new liturgical arrangements that are generally known by the abbreviated name of the theological council that initiated them: 'Vatican II'. The principal change as far as the architecture of churches was concerned was the need for the priest to face the congregation during the celebration of the mass. New altars were built Westwards of their old positions, and in some cases old furnishings

Discovering the parish church

were removed. As a result, a traditional Catholic church sometimes has more common features with a contemporary Anglo-Catholic one than a modernized Roman Catholic church.

Non-Anglican Protestant churches

Just as Roman Catholic churches are very similar to Anglo-Catholic ones, the churches of the other main Protestant movements, such as the Baptists, the Methodists and the United Reformed Church, will closely resemble those of the evangelical Anglicans. The most important part of worship in all these cases will be hearing the address by the preacher, and communal singing is a major part of services. An auditorium-type arrangement is thus preferred, and it is comparatively easy to adapt an existing structure built for another purpose. Old cinemas, for example, have sometimes become Protestant churches.

Adult membership of a Baptist church requires immersion in water, and a church may well have a permanent pool; the rite of baptism itself is highly significant. Baptist churches, along with those of the smaller Protestant sects, are given biblical and geographical names such as 'Zion' or 'Bethesda' rather than a dedication to a saint.

The language of churches

Now that you are familiar with the basic layout and functions of the parish church, you can be said to have learned the essential 'grammar' of the language of these buildings. From now onwards you will find it much easier to appreciate the beauty and variety of this language as it is expressed in the wealth of historical and artistic artefacts you can find inside. These are in a sense the 'adjectives and adverbs', and the colourful idioms, of English churches, and they are what often give them their unique and poetic character.

The following chapters will introduce you to this next stage in three ways. Firstly, you will discover how easy it is to find out about the life and history of a community from what you find in and around a church; and secondly you will learn how to decode the many scenes, emblems and faces you can find represented there in windows and sculpture. Finally, the concluding chapter will take you out of the parish to show you how the language of churches is a truly international one, and how you can use your knowledge to appreciate and interpret some of the most inspiring buildings that the Western world has produced.

CHAPTER FOUR

Local history and the church

THE PARISH church is a mine of information about the life of a community. Apart from the many personal memorials you will find both inside and in the churchyard, the fabric of the building and the changes made to it will tell a unique story about its history.

LEFT The churchyard at St Julian's, Kingston Buci, West Sussex.

The setting of the church

THE LOCATION of a church can itself indicate special historical circumstances. Until the late Middle Ages or Tudor era, it was likely to be one of only two buildings of any substance in a village – the other being the manor house.

In some cases, the owner of the manor was the patron of the benefice and lived directly alongside his parish church. Some of these manorial churches can still be found: there is a particularly fine example at Great Chalfield in Wiltshire. In rare examples, the church is actually physically attached to the house as if it were a private chapel.

The parish church at Great Chalfield in Wiltshire, left, was built immediately adjacent to the manor house, home of the parish patron.

Local history and the church

There are other situations where a church was once part of a larger complex but remains the only, or major, part left standing. The most common situation where this occurred is where the church was once part of a monastic complex.

- At **Howden** in Yorkshire the nave and transepts of the massive collegiate church of St Peter and St Paul became a parish church while the rest of the building fell into ruins. An unusual surviving stone pulpitum is a reminder that this was once more than just an average parish church.
- At **Lanercost** in Cumbria the North aisle alone of the magnificent Augustinian priory was made into a parish church; about 200 years later, the ruined nave was restored and added to it.

In other situations the church was part of a castle complex: this was the case at Kilpeck in Herefordshire, where the beautiful Norman church with its fine and expressive ornamental carving was once attached to a castle of which almost nothing remains (see page 42). In circumstances such as these you may find that masonry from the vanished building was long ago recycled for new houses nearby.

In a similar way, perhaps, there are many churches which stood at the centre of a village; the village has disappeared, but the church has remained. Perhaps a plague, a flood, or a landslip took away the inhabitants of the place and their abandoned houses eventually fell down. In some well-known cases landlords who owned a village rebuilt it elsewhere, leaving the church behind. This happened particularly during the eighteenth-century fashion for what were called 'improvements', a term specifically used to mean making alterations to the landscape simply to improve the view, especially from the manor house itself. Sometimes, as at Nuneham Courtenay in Oxfordshire, a church was rebuilt too; on other occasions it was left as an 'eye-catcher' or to emphasize the proprietorial relationship between a landowner and a church.

You will also discover churches that found themselves in the wrong place as the parish they were intended to serve began to grow. A very clear example of this can be seen on the Isle of Thanet on the north-east coast of Kent. Here the Norman and mediaeval churches in the three parishes of St John's Margate, St Peter and St Lawrence were all built a short distance inland. With the arrival in the early nineteenth century of the fashion for sea bathing, all three parishes found themselves inundated with summer visitors who would naturally expect to attend church services. The result was the construction in each case of a new church built much closer to the sea. Holy Trinity church was built in Margate; another Holy Trinity was

Many new
churches were
needed for
expanding resort
towns in the early
nineteenth
century. This is St
Peter's, a
commissioners'
church in
Brighton.

constructed at Broadstairs – the recently developed coastal part of St Peter's; and the splendid church of St George went up in Ramsgate, seawards of St Lawrence.

Both the Margate and Ramsgate buildings were commissioners' churches (see page 109). Such was the mid-Victorian enthusiasm for church building in seaside resorts that in Ramsgate by the end of the nineteenth century there were seven Anglican churches; in Brighton and Hove there were over 20. The date and splendour of a church is likely to be an indication of a period of local economic prosperity.

Sometimes a church's location derived from a direct connection with the saint to whom it was dedicated: this seems to have been the case mainly in the Celtic parts of south-west England and Wales where the saint concerned was a local figure and may even have founded the original church there themselves (see page 164). Elsewhere, sites were chosen that had mystic significance. Some early churches were founded in places which had been the scene of pagan worship, or where natural geographical features such as wells or hill tops were important to a local population.

The mediaeval village was not necessarily a clearly defined group of houses: in some cases a parish might be made up of a few homes that straggled across lanes at some

Local history and the church

Making church bells

Bells are cast from an alloy of copper and tin. A core mould is created using clay (and, for the larger bells, brickwork) to form the inner surface of the bell, and then a second mould, known as a cope, is fitted around it. The molten alloy is poured between the two moulds. Once the alloy has hardened and the moulds have been removed, the bell can be tuned by reducing the thickness of the metal.

The Whitechapel Bell Foundry in the East End of London has created some of the world's most famous bells, including Big Ben for the Palace of Westminster and the Liberty Bell in Philadelphia. The foundry has been in existence since the 1570s, and for

A view of the Whitechapel Bell Foundry.

well over 500 years it has been supplying churches in Britain; in recent centuries its bells have been sent across the world. Over the years some well-known cathedral bells, including some at Lincoln, Liverpool and St Paul's Cathedral in London, have been made at Whitechapel.

The largest bell in England can be found at St Paul's; known as 'Great Paul', it was cast in Loughborough in 1881 by John Taylor & Company. Many churches are proud of their bells and have active societies of bell ringers, sometimes known as 'campanologists'.

One of the Bow Bells of St Mary le Bow, a church by Sir Christopher Wren that was rebuilt following destruction in the Second World War.

Some churches are located far from any village but near an important crossroads or on a commanding site. This is Brentor church, Dartmoor, Devon.

distance from one another. Here churches might be built at an important crossroads or on through-routes between clusters of houses rather than at any one main centre. This is the case, for example, at the villages of Stocking Pelham, Brent Pelham and Furneux Pelham in Hertfordshire. In some cases groups of villages similarly share a name and their centres are differentiated only by the name of the church attached to it: east of Norwich, you can find Moulton St Mary and Moulton St Michael, and to the west, Rockland St Peter and Rockland All Saints. Elsewhere, as in the case of Clyst St Mary and Clyst St Lawrence in Devon, the church's dedication simply differentiates between places with a common local place name.

The churchyard

COMMUNAL burial sites have a much older history than churches, and pre-existing ones may have been consecrated with the arrival of Christianity. At all events, churchyards carry in their layout and details many signs of mystical beliefs.

In some rare cases in England and particularly in Wales circular churchyards have survived; they probably indicate a pagan past. In a very few cases pre-Christian carvings have been discovered. If the level of the churchyard rises above that of the immediately surrounding area, it may be that it has been changed by many centuries of burial. One further ancient feature of a churchyard is the yew, a long-living evergreen tree considered by some to be a symbol of rebirth or resurrection that dates from pre-Christian times.

Mediaeval city churches also had their own graveyards, and these survived until the nineteenth century when, heavily overcrowded, it was recognized that they were contaminating local water supplies. In some cases they were literally crammed with

A well-tended country churchyard.

bodies. A famous poem by Thomas Hardy recalls the time he spent in the mid-1860s as a young architect surveying the ancient churchyard of St Pancras to the north of central London so that part of the land could be bought by the Midland Railway for their route into the station that bears the same name:

> We late-lamented, resting here,
> Are mixed to human jam

When ancient churchyards were disturbed or built over, bodies were transferred elsewhere and gravestones were moved. New cemeteries – graveyards unattached to churches – were planned in suburban areas for subsequent burials, and therefore many well-known Victorian Londoners found their last resting place in modern sites at Highgate, Kensal Green or West Norwood, far from the centre. The churchyard at St Pancras itself was further encroached upon by recent works for the Eurostar route, and today it and its church provide a fascinating palimpsest of development, redevelopment and restoration across almost 1,500 years.

A lychgate marks the start of the ceremonial route into the church.

The Christian churchyard

The building of a church on an existing or new site resulted in a new set of structures and conventions. Perhaps the best-known new convention was that the North side of a church, in the shadow of the building, should be reserved for criminals and the unbaptised. The principal consecrated area of the churchyard was to the South, and bodies were traditionally buried 'facing' (that is, with their head towards) the east.

On entering the churchyard you might pass through a lychgate, a mediaeval tradition that was enthusiastically revived in Victorian times. The purpose of it was to provide shelter for the funeral procession as it arrived at the churchyard and waited for the parson to come out to commence the service there. It consists of a gate with a small roof, and, in rare cases, a surviving platform for the coffin; more frequently you will find a bench which can be used for sitting on. Some late mediaeval examples with very fine timberwork have survived: possibly the oldest in England is the late fifteenth-century example at Boughton Monchelsea in Kent; that at Ashwell in Hertfordshire is of a similar date. The lychgate at Anstey, also in Hertfordshire, is combined with a lock-up for troublesome parishioners. You will find that recent lychgates were often built as gifts in memory of a local resident.

Churchyard crosses

A Celtic cross outside Iona Abbey, on the west coast of Scotland.

The second architectural feature of the churchyard may well be a cross. Timber crosses were originally planted to mark a place of worship in a village before the church itself was built; in time they were replaced with stone ones. Some of the earliest stone crosses have survived in Wales and Cornwall, and in a few other sites in the north of England. The former are sometimes in the ancient form of a Celtic cross – that is, a cross superimposed upon a circle.

In mediaeval times a stone 'cross' was sometimes erected in a churchyard as a memorial to all those buried there. This was not necessarily cross-shaped: most seem to have had heads in the form of a tabernacle or decorated box in gothic style, ornamented with figures representing Jesus or Mary. In most cases the exact form of the tabernacle is unknown because so many were destroyed for religious reasons during or after the Reformation; an old shaft itself might remain in part. There would have been crosses or tabernacles in the streets and markets of English towns similar to those often found today in the Roman Catholic countries of Europe, but they were eradicated almost entirely in the wake of the Reformation.

Processions and other ceremonies traditionally took place around stone crosses, particularly on Palm Sunday – the feast that falls on the Sunday before Easter and which commemorates Jesus' triumphal entry into Jerusalem before his trial and execution. The revival of historic ceremonial in the nineteenth-century Church was a reason why crosses, like lychgates, reappeared in Victorian times. They nearly always have three steps at their bases, and thus naturally provide a raised platform for preachers.

The war memorial

An English churchyard will very often have a war memorial, erected during the First World War (1914–18) and added to during the Second (1939–45). These memorials provide a telling insight into the losses of the parish during wartime; you will note that the number of military casualties during the First World War was nearly always not only much greater than in the Second, but also that a large proportion of local families were directly affected. Reading the names will give an immediate and touching picture of the extent to which a community was involved in the war; it may well inadvertently provide the names of the largest families in a village. Prominent villagers or church patrons sometimes contributed these memorials as a personal gift to commemorate the loss of a son or other relative. Some memorials are located within the church itself.

A war memorial outside St Mary's Parish Church in Rawtenstall.

There may be graves for individual war casualties in a parish churchyard, and in some towns they may be in a separate enclosure. The headstones of graves established by the Commonwealth War Graves Commission will share a uniform design that was agreed upon following the First World War, and which can also be seen in the large military cemeteries across Europe. In England these graves are tended by individual contractors by agreement with the Commission.

Gravestones and tombs

In books and films churchyards have always been associated with carved-stone graveyards and overgrown tombs. In fact in recent times a number of accidents with collapsing memorials have resulted in the practice whereby gravestones are laid flat on the ground; if this continues, it will radically change the appearance of the churchyard.

Gravestones provide those interested in local history with a great deal of information: the birth and death dates of villagers, great and humble, can be found where the elements have not made inscriptions indecipherable. The wording of these inscriptions varies greatly from one period to the next, and there is much to be gained by identifying the various parts of the same churchyard that were developed at different times. Eighteenth-century memorials tend to have a philosophical tone to them, often adapting popular and somewhat wry sayings, including the well-known verse:

> Behold me now as ye pass by
> as you are now so once was I
> as I am now so you must be
> Therefore prepare to follow me.

On the other hand, Victorian graves usually carry more sentimental messages, with quotations or verses derived from the New Testament or the hymnal: typical examples might include:

Family tombs

Some of the most remarkable examples of tombs in parish churches are those of successive generations of leading families. Perhaps the most famous of all of these are at St Mary's, Warwick, the parish church of the Beauchamp and Neville families who dominated English politics for over a hundred years during the Middle Ages. Effigies of Thomas Beauchamp, first Earl of Warwick and Knight of the Garter, and his wife lie on a magnificent tomb that is surrounded by alabaster figures. Perhaps even more remarkable is the tomb of Richard Beauchamp, who died in 1439 leaving a will that requested the building of a chapel in which he would eventually rest. He is represented by a bronze effigy, with a griffin and a bear at his feet, and is surrounded below by gilded figures in delicate carved niches. Later tombs in the church include that of Robert

The effigy of Richard Beauchamp at St Mary's, Warwick.

Dudley, Earl of Leicester and the early favourite of Queen Elizabeth I.

Other dynastic collections of tombs can be found in churches closely associated with prominent families. At Chenies in Buckinghamshire you can find the nineteen memorials of the Russell family, the Dukes of Bedford, who chose to continue to be buried here even after the construction of a new sepulchral crypt in the Victorian church close to their estate at Woburn. Even more members of the Spencer family are buried in the North chapel of St Mary's at Great Brington in Northamptonshire; the group excludes the late Diana, Princess of Wales, however: she was buried on a small island on the family estate at Althorp. The finest of these dynastic collections of tombs were erected in the sixteenth and seventeenth centuries, some by famous sculptors of their day, including Joseph Nollekens and Francis Chantrey. Other important family mausoleums include the de Veres at Bures in Suffolk, which dates back to the late thirteenth century; the Howards, at Framlingham in Suffolk, which includes the tomb of a bastard son of Henry VIII who married into the family; the Vincents at Stoke d'Abernon in Surrey, where a painted seventeenth-century Lady Vincent reclines in fashionable full dress; the Berkeleys, at Berkeley in Gloucestershire; and the Marneys at Layer Marney in Essex, where Henry Marney lies under an unusual ornamental canopy.

Sometimes it is the effigies themselves that can be the most affecting. In the twelfth-century round Temple Church in London there is a large although somewhat decayed collection of figures of knights (see pages 60–1); there is a similar collection, of members of the de la Beche family, at Aldworth in Berkshire. The composed face and elaborate hairstyle of Elizabeth de Strelley, at All Saint's, Strelley, in Nottinghamshire, are unforgettable. Occasionally one comes across highly realist portrait-tableau compositions. At Quainton in Buckinghamshire there is an early eighteenth-century example that shows a judge and his wife in mourning for their young son.

The tradition continued right up to the twentieth century: at Mells in Somerset there is a striking equestrian portrait sculpture by Alfred Munnings, on a plinth designed by Edwin Lutyens. Ninian Comper designed a beautiful mediaeval-style tomb for St Alban's in Holborn.

Lord Thou knows I loved the habitation of Thy house
His end was Peace, Perfect Peace.

A person's achievements and public positions may be recorded; this together with the proximity of other family graves can give a vivid picture of their role and prominence in village life; additionally, the local historian will often be interested to discover a record of the common surnames of a parish.

A number of symbols used in gravestones – in particular, skulls, and cherubs' heads with wings – were used for hundreds of years. In some churchyards the same designs were used many times over, quite possibly by a dynasty of stonemasons. People at all periods have chosen unusual inscriptions: a recent grave at Barham in Kent simply quotes from the biblical Book of Proverbs: 'Look to the ant thou sluggard'. The name of the deceased is not given, but no doubt former neighbours will long remember who is buried there.

Roman Catholic churchyards can be particularly interesting for the local historian because their memorials may well be to those who have come to Britain from abroad with their own traditions. At St Augustine's church in Ramsgate, for example, several families of Italian immigrants have built memorials in a Continental style, with florid inscriptions and photographic portraits of the deceased. The churchyard also contains tombs of foreign sailors whose bodies were rescued from the English Channel directly beyond its walls. The graveyard of a small Roman Catholic church in a large city might contain memorials to surprisingly prominent people. In the case of St Thomas of Canterbury, in Fulham to the west of central London, for example, you can find the graves of two famous church architects: Joseph Hansom (who also invented the hansom cab); and Herbert Gribble, who designed the splendid neo-classical Brompton Oratory in Kensington.

Using the churchyard

In addition to its various liturgical and commemorative uses, a churchyard may well have been the only accessible and maintained common area in a village and the massive church walls will have been useful for various purposes. The churchyard may therefore have been used for distinctly non-religious activities, including games and sports of all kinds. Prominent among these was archery, which was compulsory for male villagers in the late Middle Ages.

The first neo-classical parish church in England

St Paul, Covent Garden, London

THE IMPOSING portico of St Paul's church is a familiar sight for visitors to Covent Garden market, and for many it is by far the most important building in a part of London crammed with fascinating historical remains. It was originally designed by Inigo Jones, the architect who introduced the Italian neo-classical style to England, and in spite of alterations and improvements over the centuries it is still redolent of the sophisticated tastes of the Stuart court.

Kings and queens had long resisted pressure to develop the rural areas around the historic cities of London and Westminster, but in 1630 the Earl of Bedford finally managed to gain permission to build a square here. Charles I gave his approval on condition that the earl erected a fine urban monument that would rival the latest continental designs. A piazza – a novelty in England – was created with arcaded terraces to the north and east, and a church to the west. The terraces have long been replaced, but the church, although refaced, remains.

According to legend, the earl was reluctant to pay for too splendid a church – a loss-maker in what was otherwise a speculative, commercial development. A barn would do, he said; so Jones promised him 'the handsomest barn in England'. And indeed the church is spatially simple – a single interior space – and was originally built of rendered brick. Its detailing is austere rather than following the contemporary Italian fashion for luxuriant 'mannerist' styles. It has its surprises, however; the appearance of a great door facing the market is illusory, because this is the position of the east-facing altar inside; and the true entrance is through the churchyard to the north and south (see more about liturgical geography on pages 88–9). The church remains one of London's handsomest landmarks.

History within the church

Spectacular churches were built thanks to the thriving fifteenth-century wool trade. The steeple at Louth in Lincolnshire is the tallest of any English parish church.

THE CHURCH building itself, of course, will often be a wonderful repository for those looking for traces of local history. Much of this will come in the form of tombs, memorials and inscriptions of various kinds, but it is important to realize that the building itself and its present-day condition will have a great deal to tell about the changing times it has seen.

Much of this is the consequence of historical events that you have already encountered. In the first place, a period of prosperity will leave its mark on churches. The splendid Perpendicular churches of East Anglia, built when the wool and cloth trade were at their peak in the fifteenth century, can seem almost like cathedrals when compared

The English Civil War and the Interregnum

The English Civil War, which also affected Scotland, Wales and Ireland, was a highly traumatic event for the Church of England, its parsons and its parish congregations everywhere. The war broke out in 1642 when parliament disputed King Charles I's right to impose taxes without its approval, and after the king and his Church leaders had sought to influence the procedures of the judicial courts. The Long Parliament, so called because it sat for 20 years, raised troops to confront the king. England divided between Charles' supporters, known as Royalists, and supporters of parliament, or Parliamentarians, and for nine years the nation was wracked with conflict.

There were two military phases to the Civil War: the first began in 1642, and continued over a series of mainly inconclusive battles won by either side until the king was defeated at Naseby in Northamptonshire by Thomas Fairfax's New Model Army in June 1645. The following year Charles in effect capitulated. The underlying constitutional problems were not resolved, however, and when Royalist rebellions threatened the army's control, a second round of fighting broke out. Charles, accused of treason, was sentenced to death and executed in January 1649. Oliver Cromwell, member of parliament for Cambridge and now the leading military commander, assumed power in place of the king and became Lord Protector. Until his death in 1658 Cromwell ruled without an elected parliament. He was succeeded by his son Richard, who was soon supplanted by army leaders. A successful invasion of England in 1660 by General Monck, the English commander of the Scottish army, was aimed at restoring an elected government and resulted in the election of a new parliament which almost immediately invited Charles I's son, Charles II, to return from exile and assume the throne.

The War is as significant to Church history as it is to political history even though its effect was confused. Cromwell and some of the parliamentary leaders were Puritans, and part of their aim was to overthrow the bishops, redistribute their incomes, and crush any remnants of Catholic ritual. But the War and Interregnum failed to install a coherent alternative system to that which had existed previously, and such reforms as were achieved, including the criminalizing of the celebration of Christmas and of travelling on Sundays, were broadly unpopular. Relations between the army, parliament, the various religious factions, and the angry and poor city mobs were constantly unstable. More church architecture and fittings were destroyed than during the Reformation. Charles II's Church reverted to the pre-War model, and it was left to philosophers and scientists, such as John Locke, Thomas Hobbes, William Harvey and Isaac Newton, to create the intellectual conditions that were eventually more seriously to undermine the Church's authority.

to the typical small country church. The steeple at Louth, in Lincolnshire and on the borders of the region, is the tallest of any England parish church, and the famous 'Stump' of the church at Boston to the south of the county is the tallest parish church tower. The combination of different local styles of building and the fact that prosperity came to different regions at different times all mean that the best churches in any one area of the country are likely to provide a kind of commentary on local fortunes. Thus these magnificent constructions to the East of England advertised not only the power of the Church but more specifically the prosperity of the competing merchants who were paying for the buildings, and their historical value is enriched by the names, mottoes and effigies of the merchants that can be found all over them (see page 159).

Protestants and Puritans

It will already be clear that the Reformation resulted in changes being made to churches throughout England. The communion table replaced the altar; the pulpit began to become a more central fixture; and many images of saints were destroyed or whitewashed over. Stained-glass windows, too, were removed if they were considered problematic according to Protestant principles.

This was not, however, the only wave of architectural destruction that churches faced, and quite possibly it was not the worst. The mid-seventeenth-century English Civil War had a disastrous effect on English churches (see pages 151–2). The early Stuart Church, particularly under archbishop William Laud, was not as strictly Protestant as the Church had been during Edward VI's reign, and the Puritans who supported Cromwell and his Parliamentary troops were doubly keen to see eradicated all traces of what they considered as a relapse into superstitious worship. In addition this was, unlike the Reformation period, a military conflict in which troops moved about the country taking control of towns and villages, sometimes using churches or cathedrals as temporary barracks. Fittings – in particular mediaeval stained glass and statues – that had survived the Reformation were vandalized, this time often gratuitously. The mediaeval west front of Lichfield cathedral with its fine arrangements of statues was a particularly tragic victim of the English Civil War. By way of contrast, the Restoration to the English throne of King Charles II in 1660 led to the development of a cult of his father, the executed Charles I, and some chapels were dedicated to him. The best known of these is at Tunbridge Wells in Kent.

Naturally the impact of both the Reformation and the English Civil War on churches varied according to local support and circumstances. The Puritans were strongest in East Anglia, around Cromwell's homeland, and consequently churches were altered there with the support of local clergy. If substantial decorative mediaeval work has survived in a church, it is a sign that the parish succeeded in passing through the era unscathed, or perhaps that a resourceful parson was able to protect church property.

The English Civil War probably damaged more churches than the Reformation had done, as gratuitous military damage was added to religious iconoclasm.

Evidence of the lack of religious toleration can be seen in more discreet ways. Members of religious minorities sometimes left Britain for the Americas where they could continue their practices in relative freedom. Their descendants have since returned to commemorate their ancestors with memorial tablets. At Southwark cathedral in London there is a chapel in honour of John Harvard, a seventeenth-century parishioner who left England with fellow Puritans in 1637 during William Laud's archbishopric and subsequently endowed Harvard University. In many smaller churches you can find monuments to the families of Englishmen who became famous abroad: at St Mary Redcliffe in Bristol (see page 102) there is a memorial to William Penn, the father of the founder of Philadelphia – as well as a whalebone that is thought to have been brought back from Newfoundland by John Cabot.

Altering churches

A church is the ideal place to identify the busy and the quiet times in the history of the parish. You have already discovered that the Victorians built and rebuilt churches on a scale unknown since the Middle Ages. It is usually not hard to discover when

Local history and the church

Redundant churches

MANY HUNDREDS of churches have outlived their original function; usually this is because of a decline in church-going among the general public, but it also happens because populations have moved elsewhere. In 1983 the Church of England adopted a procedure, a pastoral measure with the force of an act of parliament, whereby these buildings can be demolished, converted, or retained as historical monuments.

This current procedure is a sophisticated one that requires consultation not only with a parochial church council but also with members of the public and interested bodies such as the local planning authority. An important participant in the process is the Church Commissioners, the body that manages the national assets of the Church.

Once closure is agreed, the church building passes into the hands of the local diocese which is then required to find an alternative use for the building. The decision on this is taken following further consultation with national church bodies. When a building is sold there will be special arrangements for removing human remains, tombs,

memorials or other contents, and covenants may be drawn up to prevent inappropriate future uses and to ensure access to monuments. The Churches Conservation Trust takes over the care of disused churches which are to be preserved as architectural monuments.

When churches that are listed buildings are scheduled for conversion or demolition, the Church is expected to consult with recognized amenity societies in order to get the opinion of architectural historians and knowledgeable enthusiasts as to their proposed treatment. There are four national societies that between them cover historical buildings: the Society for the Protection of Ancient Buildings, which is concerned with buildings up to the eighteenth century; the Georgian Group; the Victorian Society; and the Twentieth Century Society. These have professional caseworkers that can inspect and report on cases under consideration, and committees which meet regularly to formulate decisions that are forwarded to the relevant parties.

The question of redundancy is likely to be a sensitive one, not least for architectural enthusiasts. Sometimes, and quite often in the cases of resort towns that have far too many church buildings for modern uses, it sometimes seems frustrating that architecturally distinguished churches are closing while their less interesting neighbours are still attracting large congregations. This is not, of course, something that can reasonably be changed, but the Church is always under pressure to demonstrate to amenity groups that it has a measured and informed policy of closure.

A former church now in use as a pub.

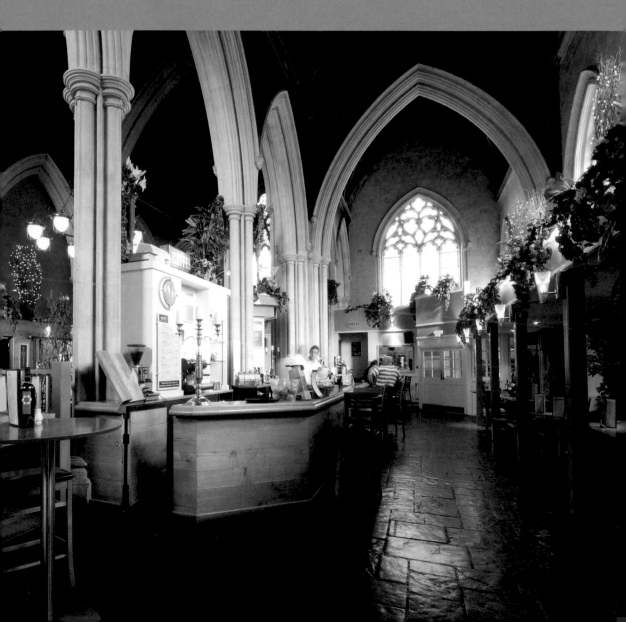

the major period of restoration took place because not only the fabric of the building but also some of the major fittings inside will have been replaced. The arrival of
an enthusiastic young parson, typical of the reforming religious movements of the
early and mid-nineteenth century, will mark a new stage in the life of a church and
also very often the point at which a poor, straggling village was transformed into a
literate and (outwardly, at any rate) pious community.

The process continues today – in a different way of course. While some churches
are being declared redundant and are demolished, converted, or transferred to the
care of the Churches Conservation Trust, others are growing (see page 155). At the
present time, very large additions have been built or are planned to many churches,
especially around London. The evangelical movement in the Church of England
now again has large, young congregations which either require changes to the traditional layout of a church, or new buildings for communal activities. It is these
congregations which have been at the forefront of the recent internal changes to
buildings that you are likely to have already seen: for example, the building of a
communion table Westwards of its traditional place. The current period may well
prove to be an important one for the social historians of the future.

Any alteration to the built fabric or the fittings of a church has always required
a special form of permission called a faculty. This is today granted by the chancellor
of a diocese on the basis of a recommendation from the diocesan advisory
committee (DAC). The chancellor is a lawyer, usually a highly experienced one,
who advises a diocesan bishop; the DAC will include architectural historians and
other church experts, and will discuss applications for alterations, for example the
installation of a new memorial or the moving of a communion table, on the basis of
a submission from an incumbent and of comments from parishioners or other interested parties. In problematic cases an appeal might be made to a diocesan consistory
court, which is a higher authority and is usually presided over by the chancellor.

One of the most popular requests made to DACs today is also one of the most
controversial for architectural historians: the subdivision of the church into smaller
spaces which can be used for church-related activities or to provide lavatories or
kitchen space. In one recent case an application was lodged to provide space for a
tiny post-office counter. A parish hall which might otherwise have been able to house
some of these new facilities may well have been let to raise money, and the church may
be located so that an extension is unfeasible; at the same time, the nave is rarely filled to
capacity and may be difficult to heat, and so subdivision seems a practical if aesthetically

problematic solution. By reading the newsletters of architectural amenity groups, such as the Society for the Protection of Ancient Buildings or the Victorian Society, it is possible to see which churches are currently under discussion and to read the pros and cons of the argument for their alteration.

Nearly all pre-Victorian churches and many later ones are listed buildings, which means that they are considered to have national historical or architectural interest. Church buildings, however, are exempt from the normal process of seeking listed building consent from the local planning authority. Instead, permission must be sought through the DAC as for any other alteration, but in this case amenity societies may submit their own professional opinion to the committee. Since 1994 other Churches have also been exempt from the conventional listed building process providing they follow a reasonable procedure for making a decision. Individual cathedrals and churches may now enter heritage partnership agreements with local authorities and with English Heritage, the government body responsible for historic buildings.

The existence of faculties from all periods can be of great interest to historians because they will record changing attitudes not only to architectural style but, perhaps just as importantly, to traditions of liturgy and worship.

This communion table has been moved Westwards towards the nave, creating a modern worship space.

Personal memorials

THE MOST powerful memorials to individuals in a parish are often the tombs that can be found in churches. It is also the case that some highly ornamental memorials are rich with valuable details about the lives of the deceased – not just in the form of inscriptions but also in the way that they are depicted. The clothing and the inclusion of objects that were associated with them, or are symbolic of their life and achievements, can all reveal a great deal.

You have seen that in mediaeval times special memorial chapels called chantries were erected within churches in order that priests could regularly pray for the souls of the departed. These included tombs which were often ornamental and included a figure of the deceased. Perhaps surprisingly the idea of the ornamental, figurative tomb survived the Reformation, and some of the most remarkable of all family memorials were erected in the Stuart and early Hanoverian eras. These can show a figure of the person commemorated not merely lying down but sitting, writing or praying. A group of churches in the prosperous area to the west of London has a truly outstanding collection of memorials of this type. These include St Dunstan's, Cranford, close to Heathrow Airport, which has several, including a massive one to Sir Roger Aston depicting him at

An Easter sepulchre (see page 98).

The serene poise of a perfect Wren interior

St Stephen Walbrook, London

IT SEEMS likely that some of the 51 churches attributed to Sir Christopher Wren in the City of London were in fact designed by his assistants because their quality and originality varies considerably. In a handful of cases, however, there can be no doubt that you are looking at the work of a genius. St Stephen Walbrook, built from 1672–80, is one of these. In fact it is known that Wren was paid 20 guineas for taking special care in its design.

The exterior of the church is unassuming, so the elegance of its interior comes as a surprise. Once through the entrance doors, Wren's brilliant design immediately becomes apparent – as can easily be appreciated by a visit to the church's website and its 360° view (http://ststephenwalbrook.net). The architect was required by the liturgical conventions of the day to design a longitudinal nave with an altar at the East end; he wanted at the same time to try out the centralized baroque forms that were becoming fashionable in Europe. No doubt he also wanted to experiment on a small scale with ideas he had in mind for the new cathedral of St Paul's. This small church brilliantly combines the East-West orientation with a prominent dome that clearly dominates the centre of the nave. The fusion is achieved by supporting the dome on a ring of concave spandrels above a network of Corinthian columns. It seems to be floating.

Unfortunately Wren's subtle design has been compromised by a reordering that has placed an altar by Henry Moore (and this clearly is an altar, not a communion table) under the dome: it has popularly been likened to a large piece of Camembert cheese. Nevertheless, the remarkable space all around remains one of the great treasures of London's architecture. Never were 20 guineas so well spent.

Sir Roger Aston facing his two wives at prayer on his memorial at Cranford in Middlesex.

prayer under a large renaissance-style arch with his two wives and five daughters. At nearby St Giles', Ickenham, there is a well-known memorial which depicts the infant Robert Clayton, who died in 1665, wrapped in realistic swaddling clothes. The most splendid memorials from the early part of the eighteenth century are often to army or naval commanders and have large collections of trophies – that is, arrangements of weapons, bugles, standards and other military hardware of a practical or symbolic kind. The realism of the clothing depicted in these memorials is of great interest, and contrasts with that of the stylized apparel sometimes seen in large Victorian memorials which consciously imitated mediaeval originals.

Local history and the church

Other memorials can also tell us about past fashions. For many hundreds of years ornamental brass plates were affixed to tombs or memorials in churches, and a large number of these have survived. The most interesting include clear depictions of soldiers, noblemen and women, and members of the clergy in sufficient detail to be able to make out the details or their dress. Family heraldry, which often included ornamental collars and animals such as small lions or dogs lying at their feet, will give information regarding their status and local importance (see pages 201–3). Occasionally various accoutrements of the deceased person's profession or rank were added. Inscriptions tend to be small and may be quite difficult to read, although the name and the date or age at death in Roman numerals can often be made out. Sometimes a further text, usually a religious supplication, issues from the person's mouth in the form of a scroll. The Reformation resulted in the mutilation or destruction of many brasses, so what you see today may well be only part of the original design, or a reconstruction.

As they did with much else of mediaeval origin, the Victorians revived ornamental brasses: Augustus Pugin, the leader of the Gothic revival, designed many himself and published illustrations for others to learn from. There are at least six by him at the Roman Catholic cathedral of St Chad in Birmingham. Some well-known Victorian architects who were admirers of Pugin both designed and were commemorated by similar mediaeval-style brasses: that of Sir George Gilbert Scott (see page 121) in the nave of Westminster Abbey was designed by George Edmund Street, his former pupil and the architect of the Royal Courts of Justice in London.

Pugin's own tomb at Ramsgate, which was designed by his son Edward around 1860, is a convincing recreation of the mediaeval type and includes small effigies of his wife and children at prayer in its side panels.

Smaller monuments

A memorial does not have to be large and impressive in order to be interesting, and many small wall plaques in parish churches bear witness to fascinating characters in the past. The lengthy inscriptions that were commonplace in the eighteenth century may not perhaps always have been intended to be literally true, but they nevertheless reflect the preoccupations, concerns and values of the time. At St Mary Abbots, the parish church of Kensington in West London, a memorable tablet to Jael Boscawen, who died at the age of 82 in 1730, was kept and rehung in George Gilbert Scott's new building. It reads:

Church dedications

CHURCHES HAVE been dedicated to saints for more than 1,500 years. In the early Church a building may well have had a direct connection with a particular saint: below St Peter's in Rome remains were found of a second-century Christian martyrium, a structure for worship designed like a large tomb, which may have been built over the grave of St Peter himself. In a similar but rather more modest fashion, many churches in the Celtic parts of Britain are associated with saints so local that only one building is dedicated to them. St Mellanus at Mullion, St Maddern at Madron, and saints Mylor and Probus at the villages with those names are some of the best-known ones. Another unique dedication, St Enodoc, at an isolated spot on the north Cornish coast, is the burial place of that great lover of churches John Betjeman.

The choice of dedication may have been intended to draw upon the particular characteristics of a saint (see Chapter 5). These may have had political connotations, as dedications to saints such as Thomas of Canterbury or Charles King and Martyr suggest. Another example is that of Edmund the Martyr, an East Anglian king who was murdered by Danes in 869. His body was eventually interred in the Suffolk town which was later named after him: Bury St Edmunds.

Anglican churches can be named after things and events as well as people. At Doddington in Kent the dedication is to the Beheading of St John the Baptist.

St Francis of Assisi depicted in a stained-glass window.

She was adorned with
rare faculties of the mind, singular acuteness
sagacity and Judgement, with a generous heart,
full of piety and devotion to God, full of modesty
candor diffusive charity and universal benevolence
to mankind, beloved admired revered by all as well
as by relations as being confessedly the
ornament, and at the same time the tacit reproach
of a wicked Age.

A recent modern plaque at the other end of the same church, in the North chancel aisle, commemorates Christopher Ironside (1913–92), the designer of the first set of British decimal currency – and also of the memorial to Earl Mountbatten of Burma in Westminster Abbey. From the 1930s onwards well-known sculptors and typographical designers such as Eric Gill contributed a great deal towards the revival of memorial plaques as a form of art in its own right, and Ironside's designs continued that worthy tradition.

A modern commemorative plaque.

Other memorials

Tombs and memorial tablets are not the only ways in which the names of individuals can be recorded for posterity. Once inside a church you will soon find that there are plenty of different places in which you can find them, including:

- **Family pews**. Some churches still have enclosed seats that were designated for the use of a particular family.
- **Memorial windows**. You will find names of donors and of those commemorated inscribed either around the edges of windows or woven into their design. A window in the lady chapel at Ely cathedral continues the tradition by commemorating the department store John Lewis which had contributed to a recent restoration of the building.
- **Bells**. You are unlikely to see them, of course, but nevertheless many bells carry the names of donors. The tenor bell at Sherborne Abbey in Dorset, part of a set considered to be the heaviest peal of eight in the world, was originally given by Cardinal Wolsey in the sixteenth century; although it has been recast several times, his name is still inscribed on it.
- **Church plate**: the gold or silver dishes and wine chalice used at the service of holy communion, as well as dishes used in baptism, altar crosses and candlesticks. Many churches have very fine plate given by individuals, and sometimes a family's coat of arms will appear on it. The design of the pieces will reflect the period in which they were made, and so naturally there is a great difference between the rather sturdy seventeenth-century examples, which generally closely resemble domestic plates and beakers, and the highly ornate, Victorian gothic revival ones.
- **Vestments**, that is, the robes worn by the clergy during a service, were often also the gifts of individuals and reflect the changing fashions of the periods. The revival of mediaeval-type vestments by Victorian churchmen for the first time since the Reformation was considered scandalous by some in their day, and there were stories of clergymen being pelted with stones or worse on their way to a service. Some cathedrals display impressive cope chests – huge wooden storage boxes in which a cope, a semicircular robe, could be stored flat.
- **Organs**. These were first installed in mediaeval times, when they were operated by pumping bellows – sometimes by large numbers of people at once. By the end of the Middle Ages organs were common in parish churches, but they were disapproved of by Puritans, and disappeared. The craft of organ building was

The nineteenth-century church revival

THE CHURCH of England during the later Georgian period was somewhat in the doldrums; many of its clergymen, especially its curates, were badly paid and poorly housed, while its bishops and well-connected parsons – sometimes called 'squarsons' since their lives resembled those of the squires –

seemed more interested in social pursuits than in preaching. Church buildings too were in a dismal state.

The reaction came from two different directions. From the late eighteenth century a group of increasingly influential evangelical Christians, whose leaders were nicknamed the Clapham Sect after

An Oxford Movement church: All Saints', Margaret Street, London.

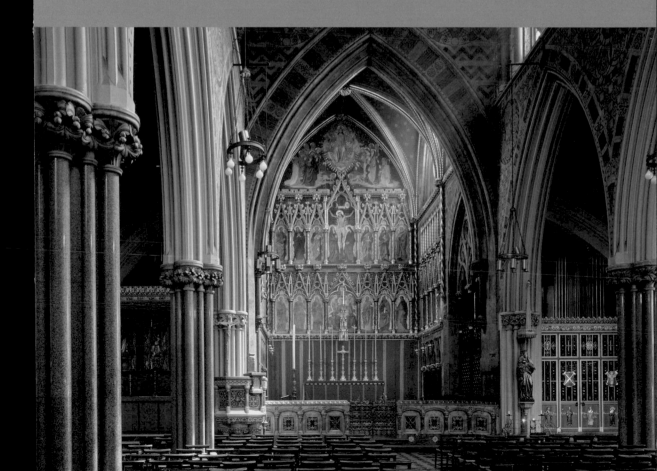

their South London base, began to press for reform. The best known among the leadership of the movement was William Wilberforce. Many young clergymen were inspired to introduce literacy, piety and abstention into the sleepy congregations of England, a process that can clearly be seen in novels about early Victorian life.

From the 1830s an alternative tendency developed: the Oxford Movement. Its leaders, who were mainly senior members of Oxford colleges, were encouraged by theologians such as Edward Pusey and John Keble to try to re-establish the ritual and appearances of the pre-Reformation Church. As part of this, they strongly supported the revival of authentic gothic architecture and fittings promoted by architects such as Pugin, Scott and Butterfield. Although they were often accused of flirting with Rome, and their best-known member John Henry Newman eventually converted to Roman Catholicism, their influence on the design of the Victorian church was immeasurable and by the end of the nineteenth century theirs was the dominant movement in the Church hierarchy.

It is the nineteenth-century revival that we have to thank for the variety and high quality of Victorian church architecture – features which can be seen in almost every town and village in the country. Church leaders recognized that a fine church building could be the best possible advertisement for the power of the Church nationally; furthermore, creating a new building could be an opportunity for parishioners, and in particular the wealthy among them, to come forward and unite in a project that would link them personally to the parish and its fortunes. At the same time, the contemporary interest among architects and critics in the 'truth' or even 'morality' of a well-built structure, as opposed to the often shabby building procedures of the previous generation, and the importance that the gothic revival attached to quality craftsmanship and expressive art works, all combined to create an atmosphere in which church building was very highly prized.

Some of the most magnificent buildings of the era were in fact the result of personal acts of devotion. The Church of the Holy Angels at Hoar Cross in Staffordshire, designed by George Frederick Bodley and Thomas Garner from 1872 and one of the most spectacular parish churches in England, was the gift of a widow named Emily Meynell-Ingram.

revived with the Restoration, and when the new St Paul's cathedral was opened in December 1697 it was with one of the finest organs in the world. In more modest churches organs were usually installed either in a West gallery or in the North chancel aisle, a position preferred by the Victorians.

Many of the fittings found in churches were made by well-known specialist manufacturers, and with practice it becomes possible to identify examples of their work.

Communal memorials

Churches may include chapels dedicated to local branches of national organizations where flags, banners and special memorials commemorate their work and play a part in special annual or occasional services. In a cathedral or large church these organizations might include local regiments; in smaller churches you may find a chapel or an area dedicated to a guild, a friendly society, the Mothers' Union, the Boy Scouts, or another charitable organization which in each case is responsible for the chapel's upkeep or is otherwise remembered there.

Some London City churches with a small number of parishioners maintain a broad connection with a particular profession: the 'printers' church' of St Bride's, Fleet Street, is today dedicated to journalists, and maintains a continually updated memorial to those recently killed or in danger while carrying out their work. St Martin-in-the-Fields, which was the first English church to broadcast a service by wireless (in 1924) and on television (in 1950), historically had an important connection with pacifism and today maintains its long-standing tradition of helping the homeless. The history of many non-ecclesiastical organizations is often inevitably closely bound up with the history of the parish church.

Commonwealth war graves in a London cemetery.

Personal memorials

CHAPTER FIVE

The decoration of a church

ALMOST every Anglican church will contain examples of design and ornament that do much more than simply demonstrate the high quality of traditional workmanship. They will reflect religious ideas and messages that are waiting to be understood. Looking for these messages and interpreting them can be one of the great pleasures of a visit.

LEFT A detail from the church of St Michael and All Angels, Brighton.

The idea of iconography

YOU WILL BY now be familiar with the types of images that churches are decorated with: in all but the most evangelical buildings they will include saints, scenes from the Bible, and local benefactors.

A detail of a window designed by Pugin depicting St Matthew (centre), flanked by St Simon (with a saw, left) and St Jude (right).

These images might be in sculpture, stained glass or decorative panels, and are sometimes part of an overall scheme that has been planned with the intention of presenting church-goers with a lesson in Christianity. The way in which groups of images are organized in order to illustrate a particular message or theme is called an iconography.

Mediaeval churches were rich in iconographical schemes but nearly all of them were destroyed during the Reformation or the English Civil War. That was because the images seemed to the Protestant reformers to be too close to idolatry: that is,

they were worried that churchgoers might worship them or confuse the idea of a holy figure with the physical representation of one. The more strict of the reformers would point to the second commandment given to Moses on Mount Sinai which instructed the people of Israel not to 'make a carved image for yourself nor the likeness of anything in the heavens above, or on the earth below, or in the waters under the earth'. In the days well before photographic images or indeed accurate likenesses were commonplace this appeared to rule out statues or portraits for any purpose – and especially for display in a church.

The influence of the strict religious interpretation of this commandment cannot be underestimated and it influenced church design for over 250 years. In some cases, the effects lasted longer still. At the presbyterian Barclay Church in Edinburgh, under construction in the 1860s, the architect was asked by the church authorities to stop his craftsmen from sculpting images of angels into the stonework of the doorways halfway through the work. As a result you can still see today figures that are only partly carved.

Nevertheless, examples of all kinds of early iconography can be found across Britain. As with much else in the churches of today, however, the best remaining iconographical schemes are in fact Victorian, and they reflect an earnest attempt to revive mediaeval traditions.

Iconographical families

The idea behind any iconographical scheme is that a set of images should trigger a particular train of thought: a figure of a saint was intended to provoke a reminder of his or her many holy attributes, or the depiction of an event could remind the onlooker of a religious or theological message. Even individual surviving images can generally be linked to one of the conventional Christian themes.

You will have noticed that the predominant subject of decorative design work, whether in glass or sculpture, is a human figure. He or she will have been chosen because of their role as a member of one of the iconographical families. The most prominent of these groups can often be clearly identified, and they include:

- **Biblical scenes** from the Old and New Testament
- **Angels** and **devils**
- Patriarchs and prophets from the Old Testament
- Apostles, evangelists and the **doctors** of the Church
- Saints, sometimes those whose personal or legendary attributes are connected with the foundation of the church or its vicinity.

Biblical scenes

For most people in the days when mediaeval churches were first built, the Bible with its many hundreds of stories was much the best known and indeed possibly the only literary anthology. From regular church attendance – compulsory from the days of Queen Elizabeth I, but widespread beforehand – they would recognize not only many of the events described in the Bible but also understand the lessons that preachers liked to draw from them.

Some biblical events might seem more suitable for decorative schemes than others because of the colourful figures and landscapes involved in them. In fact, however, church builders preferred scenes that reinforced one of the most important beliefs of Christianity: the idea that the life of Jesus was foretold in the Old Testament, and that certain Old Testament events point directly to his birth, his work and to his death. Therefore some events were more commonly used than others. The correct term for the use by religious artists of certain scenes to symbolize other ones is typology.

The temptation of Adam and Eve in the Garden of Eden has always been a favourite subject for stained glass artists.

The expulsion of Adam and Eve from the Garden of Eden was a popular scene of this type. By disobeying God, the parents of all the peoples in the world fell into a state of sin. According to Christianity, it was only through the intervention of Jesus that people could be redeemed from this sinful existence. Thus a depiction of a scene from the first book of the Old Testament could suggest the major theme of the first books of the New Testament.

In general, biblical scenes of sacrifice, such as the moment when Abraham nearly kills his son Isaac on a mountain top, could be readily interpreted as prefiguring the sacrifice of Jesus for the redemption of mankind. Other popular themes include that of Noah's ark, which likewise tells the story of a punishment but also of a promise of future salvation.

The decoration of a church

The parables of the New Testament

MUCH OF Jesus' teaching took the form of the telling of stories about everyday situations from which his listeners could learn about themselves and grasp simply the religious messages that he wanted to convey.

Many of the images used in these symbolic stories – which are known as parables – appear in the iconography of church decoration, and you can identify them in windows, paintings and sculptures. In some cases the objects or people illustrated will form the major theme of an artwork; elsewhere they appear around the edges or in a minor role, making a subtle reference to the lessons which are to be learned from them.

The parables are described in the gospels of the four evangelists: Matthew, Mark, Luke and John. Some parables appear in more than one gospel. Here are four familiar ones in Jesus' words from the Revised English Bible version, with the name of the book and the chapter number in which they appear:

• **The lilies of the field** (Matthew, 6): 'I tell you not to be anxious about food and drink to keep you alive and about clothes to cover your body. Surely life is more than food, the body more than clothes. Look at the birds in the sky; they do not sow and reap and store in barns, yet your heavenly Father feeds them. Are you not worth more than the birds?... Consider how the lilies grow in the fields; they do not work, they do not spin; yet I tell you, even Solomon in all his splendour was not attired like one of them.'

• **The mustard seed** (Matthew, 13): 'The kingdom of Heaven is like a mustard seed, which a man took and sowed in his field. Mustard is smaller than any other seed, but when it has grown it is taller than other plants; it becomes a tree, big enough for the birds to come and roost among its branches.'

• **The sower** (Luke, 8): 'A sower went out to sow his seed. And as he sowed, some of the seed fell along the footpath, where it was trampled on, and the birds ate it up. Some fell on rock and, after coming up, it withered for lack of moisture. Some fell among thistles, and the thistles grew up with it and choked it. And some of the seed fell into good soil, and grew, and yielded a hundredfold.'

- **The lamp** (Luke, 8): 'Nobody lights a lamp and then covers it with a basin or puts it under the bed. You put it on a lampstand so that those

who come in may see the light.' Another familiar parable is that of the **prodigal son** (Luke, 15), who returns humbly to his family after squandering his wealth with loose living. He is warmly welcomed home by his father – to the annoyance of the loyal younger brother.

A stained-glass depiction of the prodigal son, seen here wasting his money by gambling.

Story cycles

When looking for biblical stories in church windows or other decorations you will find that they are often organized into groups so that a series of related events might take up all the main lights of a large window, or each of a series of smaller windows in a chancel or aisle. A five-light window might, for example, have five different scenes of suffering and redemption in its lower parts, with complementary stories from the New Testament in the more decorative upper parts.

You will therefore see that artists sought out events that could naturally occur in groups. One very popular theme is that of the various key events during Jesus' life, or his last days on earth. The latter have been formalized into a series of events that are depicted on separate panels that are sometimes located around a church. These are called the stations

of the cross. They can nearly always be found in Roman Catholic churches but occasionally also in Anglican ones. They depict a series of events and encounters from the moment when Jesus was condemned to death up to his entombment, including the three moments when he stumbled under the weight of the cross he had to carry through the streets of Jerusalem, and also the crucifixion itself. The last days of Jesus' life are referred to as the Passion, and this on its own has been the subject of many works of art.

The twelfth scene from the stations of the cross: the death of Jesus.

Some of the most powerful images inspired directly from the Bible are the scenes of the last judgment and of Jesus seated in heaven. These are derived specifically from the powerful imagery of the final book of the New Testament, called the Revelation of John in the Church of England but the Apocalypse of St John the Divine by Roman Catholics. This book is full of colourful descriptions of the end of the world, including scenes that depict fantastical monsters. In some churches you will see an image of Jesus seated on a throne, bathed in light or surrounded by angels, as a central motif that brings together prophetical scenes from both testaments. The correct term for an image of Jesus of this kind is Christ in majesty, and it is popular both for East windows (where it emphasises the effect of morning light streaming in) and for sculptural panels above major Western doorways.

A terrifying painted scene of the last judgment, full of devils and the eternal sufferings of the wicked as foretold in the book of Revelation, is called a doom (see page 182). The traditional place for it was on the nave side of the chancel arch. In that way it was perpetually in sight of the congregation. It would also have been bathed in gloom because of the glare created by the East window. The result would have been all the more frightening to look at.

Jesus seated on his celestial throne: Christ in majesty.

Stories from the life of Jesus

CERTAIN KEY events in the life of Jesus as they are recounted by the four evangelists are commonly illustrated in church windows. They can also be found in chromolithographs and steel engravings of the religious paintings that became popular as church congregations grew more pious from the middle of the nineteenth century. These events have often provided a preacher with a subject for a sermon because they can be interpreted with great richness and many different lessons can be drawn from them. As subjects for church art they therefore provide a kind of shorthand that is intended to inspire congregations.

You are likely to encounter scenes from some of the following stories in windows or elsewhere in the church:

- The **birth of Jesus**: Jesus' birth to Mary and Joseph in a stable at Bethlehem, described in Luke, 2, is commemorated with a special service at Christmas.
- The **massacre of the innocents**: from Matthew, 2. King Herod ordered the murder of all boys aged two or under in an attempt to prevent the infant Jesus growing up into a rival for his throne. But Jesus

and his parents had already escaped to Egypt.
- **Jesus as a child in the Temple**: Jesus as a 12-year-old boy astonished the teachers of the Jewish law by debating theology with them at the Temple in Jerusalem (Luke, 2).
- The **wedding feast at Cana**: the first miracle worked by Jesus was to turn water into wine at a wedding feast at Cana, a village in Galilee (John, 2).
- The **moneychangers in the Temple**: Jesus upset the tables of moneychangers and others trading in the Temple, claiming that they had turned a sacred place into a 'robbers' cave' (Mark, 11).
- The **raising of Lazarus**: Jesus raised a man from the dead, saying 'Whoever has faith in me shall live, even though he dies' (John, 11).
- The **healing of the centurion's daughter**: in the town of Capernaum on the banks of the Sea of Galilee Jesus cured the daughter of a Roman centurion, demonstrating that faith was more important than race or tradition (Matthew, 8).
- The **sermon on the mount**: in a long and eloquent sequence

recounted across three books of Matthew (5–7) Jesus spoke to a large crowd of followers. Here he recited a series of epigrams about blessedness known as the **beatitudes**, beginning 'Blessed are the poor in spirit; the kingdom of Heaven is theirs'.

- The **feeding of the five thousand**: sometime after the sermon on the mount Jesus fed a large crowd with five loaves and two fish. The story is told in all four gospels (Matthew, 14; Mark, 6; Luke, 9; John, 6). A series of well-known events from Jesus' last days on earth are also related by all the evangelists:

- The **triumphal entry on a donkey into Jerusalem** – celebrated at Palm Sunday.
- The **last supper** – commemorated at every holy communion.
- The **crucifixion** – commemorated at Good Friday.
- The **resurrection** – celebrated on Easter Sunday.

The wedding feast at Cana: Jesus turns water into wine (note centre of left-hand panel).

Angels and devils

Mediaeval theology classified angels into different types according to their importance and the type simply called 'angel' was actually the most junior of all. Heavenly beings were divided into three orders called choirs, and each of these choirs contained three different angelic types.

Angels have been a popular theme for artists and craftsmen of all centuries.

Members of the most senior choir are called the counsellors: they are, in order of seniority, the seraphim, the cherubim and the thrones. The first two names are derived from the Hebrew words used in the Old Testament. The second choir are the governors, sometimes called the rulers, and they consist of the dominions, virtues and powers. The third are the messengers: these consist of principalities, archangels and, finally, angels. All of these various types have specific qualities attributed to them by theologians or by tradition.

The archangels are named figures in the Bible and some of their names will be familiar, in particular Michael and Gabriel. The suffix 'el' means 'god' in Hebrew, the language of most of the Old Testament. Michael means 'who is like God' and denotes the warrior who defeated the devil; Gabriel means something like 'man of God' (the exact meaning is unclear), and is God's messenger. Two other well-known archangels are Raphael and Uriel.

BOTTOM
The devil
depicted in a
detail from a
'doom' – a
scene of the last
judgment.

NEXT PAGE
This window
depicts a Jesse
tree – an
ornamental
depiction of
Jesus' family
lineage. His
ancestors are
linked by
intertwining
branches.

Devils tend to appear in the form of monsters; sometimes you will see the scurrying figures with pitchforks to torture the wicked that have inspired cartoonists from all generations. The book of Revelation and other biblical sources describe monstrous creatures in the form of dragons, serpents and beasts so fantastic that they allow artists considerable licence in the depiction of them. This was useful when the role of the devil in a piece of church art was to balance visually the representation of a holy figure in a typological cycle. Satan himself was the master of the underworld and may have a prominent position in these scenes.

The patriarchs and prophets of the Old Testament

You will find that in many cases biblical figures are depicted on their own, occupying a whole window and sometimes standing under an ornate gothic canopy. Here you will often encounter the patriarchs of the Old Testament: Abraham, his son Isaac, and Isaac's son Jacob. The sons of Jacob, including Joseph, are also sometimes considered to be patriarchs since the twelve tribes that made up the Jewish people were descended from them. The term implies not only that these men were tribal leaders: it is also a reminder that Abraham stands at the head of the family tree that ended with Jesus himself.

A device called a Jesse tree is an illustration of the biblical line of descent described at the beginning of the New Testament in the gospel according to St Matthew. Perhaps the most famous example of a Jesse tree can be found on the North wall of the chancel of Dorchester abbey in Oxfordshire. Here the whole window has been sculpted in the form of a biblical family tree. At the bottom Jesse himself, the father of King David, lies realistically across the window sill; a figure of Jesus stands at the apex of the arch above, somewhat damaged by Cromwell's soldiers.

Since no one knows what the people who appeared in the Bible actually looked

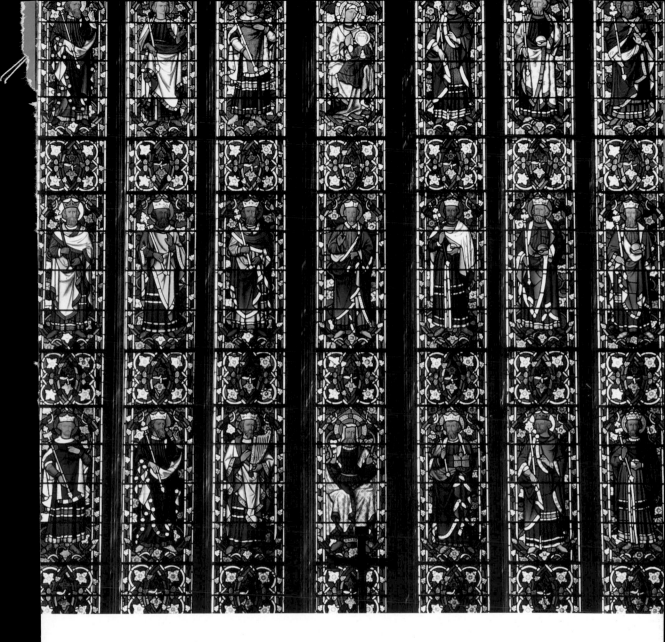

like, they needed to be identified by the inclusion of visual props that at once formed the required association in the mind of the onlooker. Sometimes, of course, you may well see their name in the form of an inscription: this was common at the time of the Victorian revival of stained glass of the 1840s because by then fewer people would have recognized the meaning of the traditional iconography.

Abraham can be identified by a knife, a reminder of his attempt to sacrifice Isaac. Similarly, the symbol for Isaac is a bundle of wood, sometimes in the form of a cross: this represents the fact that his father laid firewood in order to sacrifice him as a burnt offering, and that this intended sacrifice was a precursor of the death of Jesus on the wooden cross. This type of emblem is a clear example of how iconographers linked the Old and New Testaments through their imagery. Jacob is represented with the depiction of the sun, the moon and twelve stars, derived from a dream of his son Joseph in Genesis, 37: the stars represent the twelve sons.

Moses, the giver of the Old Testament law, is commonly seen in church iconography: he usually holds the two tablets of the law – that is, the ten commandments – that were given to him by God on Mount Sinai. Occasionally he has a pair of horns, derived from a lack of certainty about identical Hebrew words for 'to have horns' and 'to radiate light'; some artists, such as the Victorian architect William Butterfield in his highly ornate church of All Saints, near Oxford Circus in London, solved this problem by giving Moses horns that looked like rays of light!

The prophets, those who heard the word of God and who conveyed it to a usually not very sympathetic audience, include Elijah, who is signified by the chariot that took him up to heaven; Isaiah, whose symbol is a saw; Jeremiah, with a stone; and Daniel, who survived the lions' den, with a ram with four horns – another symbol derived from a mystical dream.

Other groups of Old Testament figures include royal figures such as the kings David and Solomon, and the matriarchs Sarah, Rebecca, Rachel and Leah – the wives of the patriarchs.

The evangelists, apostles and the doctors of the Church

The evangelists who wrote the gospels that open the New Testament and the apostles of the Church, the people chosen by Jesus to accompany him in his work, have a special place in all Christian iconography. Christian teachings are closely derived both from their own writings but also from interpretations of their various actions and attributes.

The four gospels written by the evangelists are slightly different from each other in content and tone, and as a result their writers – Matthew, Mark, Luke and John – have different roles to play in Christian theology. Early Christian scholars compared each one to different majestic or mythical creatures that emphasised their significance, and the symbols that represent them are derived from these ideas.

The decoration of a church

Victorian church furnishers

THE REVIVAL of the Church of England in the nineteenth century was celebrated not only with impressive new buildings but also with a rebirth of some of the ancient crafts associated with mediaeval architecture. One of the many pleasures of looking at churches is learning to identify the developing styles and characteristics of a new wave of designers.

Most of the old techniques had actually been forgotten by the 1840s, the period in which the new wave of church building began, and consequently they had to be rediscovered. Several architects of the period, in particular Augustus Pugin, worked on the design of all the traditional artefacts: not only stained glass but also tiles, metalwork and joinery. These architects encouraged the development of craft workshops that could learn the old skills. In time, manufacturers learned how to interpret the work of designers in a way that suited the style of the revived gothic architecture, and built up catalogues of standard features that could be bought for use in any church across the country.

Pugin himself built up a strong working relationship with the Birmingham ironmonger John Hardman Junior who manufactured for him the very fine items such as the door furniture and lamps that can be seen in their full splendour at, for

Victorian church furnishings were sometimes made to the highest possible standards. This spectacular pulpit and spire were designed in 1881.

did this in partnership with Herbert Minton, the innovative Staffordshire potter, and the Minton brand name still exists today. In the case of church furniture, such as the benches that were now replacing pews, several architects designed standard types that could be used anywhere.

By the later nineteenth century new stained glass workshops had become established. Possibly the best known of these was the firm of Clayton and Bell, which produced bold, vivid schemes in a strongly mediaeval style including the magnificent set of windows at the new cathedral at Truro. Towards the end of the nineteenth century the Lancaster firm of Shrigley and Hunt also established a presence, especially in the North of England.

example, the Houses of Parliament in London. Hardman later opened a stained glass studio, and Hardman glass, sometimes designed by Pugin or by his son-in-law J.H. Powell, can be found in many churches across the country. Other well-known early Victorian glass-makers include the three 'W's: Thomas Willement, William Warrington and William Wailes. Pugin also pioneered the revival of a type of mediaeval tile, called the encaustic tile, in which the design is embedded into the thickness of the material itself rather than being applied superficially. He

Perhaps the most highly regarded today of the late Victorian craft firms is Morris, Marshall, Faulkner & Co – the firm established by the great and prolific designer William Morris in 1861. Much of the glass produced by the company is striking and original, and in a style that broke away from the rigidity of typical gothic design but was intended to express mediaeval vigour and romance. Morris himself, as well as his friends Dante Gabriel Rossetti, Edward Burne-Jones and Philip Webb, were among the designers.

St John the
Evangelist
depicted with
a chalice and
dragon.

Matthew's gospel stresses the continuity of Jewish tradition in Jesus' life and so he is signified by an angel, the eternal messenger of God's word. Mark is conveyed by a winged lion, a kind of composite king of the beasts: hence the sculpture of this creature above the entrance to the church of St Mark's in Venice, where some remains of the saint are housed, and elsewhere throughout the city. Luke, a doctor, is represented by a winged ox, which is a way of comparing the death of Jesus to that of a sacrificial animal; and John is symbolized by an eagle, the bird that soars from heaven bearing the word of God.

Matthew and John were two of Jesus' twelve disciples; when they are illustrated in this role, they are denoted by symbols that are different from their evangelical ones. Here Matthew is shown by bags of money, a reference to his unpopular

Images of St Peter are easily identified by the keys that he holds.

profession as a tax collector, and John by a chalice with a serpent or dragon, which derives from a non-biblical story in which he escaped death when the poison in a drink he had been offered left the chalice in animal form. All the apostles, apart from Judas Iscariot, are saints. The number of people identified as having been apostles is actually greater than twelve, but they are always seen in groups of this number. The most commonly seen is St Peter who is easily identified by the keys of heaven that he holds. These keys have also become the symbol of the Vatican, which is ruled by the pope, who is considered by Roman Catholics to be Peter's descendant as head of the Church on earth. Perhaps the best known among the other apostles is St James the Great (or St James Major), called that to distinguish him from another, lesser, James. James' symbol is the scallop shell and he is identified with pilgrims.

The doctors of the Latin Church are the four great founding fathers of Western Christian theology: St Ambrose, a bishop; St Augustine, also a bishop and the author of an important theological text called *The City of God*; St Gregory, depicted as a pope; and St Jerome, dressed as a cardinal.

The decoration of a church

The saints

Other saints depicted in Protestant churches consist mainly of people who were killed because of their loyalty to Christianity during the first millennium. Perhaps the best known of all in England is the national patron saint, St George, whose exact history is unclear beyond the fact that he was a soldier persecuted by the Roman emperor Diocletian. He is symbolized by a dragon, or by the familiar St George's cross, and it is important not to confuse him with St Michael who can be seen slaying the devil. A figure of St Christopher is often seen in churches. His traditional place is over the entrance door from the North porch: in other words, immediately opposite those who enter through the more usual porch to the South. He was a giant, and is familiarly seen with a child, a representation of Jesus, on his shoulder.

St Christopher is the patron saint of travellers because he was said to have carried Jesus across a river, and other familiar saints are also linked with specific groups of people. St Cecilia is the patron saint of musicians, and so she might be represented with a musical instrument. St Anthony of Padua is the patron saint of the poor and can be depicted in several ways, including with a child (who might again be a representation of Jesus), with

St Andrew, a fisherman who answered Jesus' call at the Sea of Galilee.

lilies or with fish. The familiar Catherine wheel is associated with St Catherine of Alexandria who was tortured with a wheel set with knives and then beheaded in the fourth century. She is the patron saint of philosophers, in honour of her debating skills that led to her murder.

The figure of Mary, the mother of Jesus, is traditionally a much more significant figure in Roman Catholic iconography than among Protestants. She remains for many theologians a complex figure, resulting partly not so much from New Testament descriptions of her than from active attempts on the part of the Church at different times in its history to create a powerful female image in a constellation of important figures who were otherwise almost entirely male. She may be portrayed in a scene from Jesus' life, most commonly soon after his birth, and she is usually dressed in blue. Her symbols include the lily, which represents purity; in Roman Catholic churches she can be associated with the 'immaculate heart', a heart pierced by a sword. You may also find the monogram MR, from the Latin for Mary the Queen.

The Roman Catholic Church today continues to create saints; in fact Pope John Paul II created many more than any of his predecessors had done. Some of these new saints, who must be credited with having performed miracles, can be seen depicted in Catholic churches. You can also find images of figures who are recognized by the Catholic Church as being beatified, which is in effect a junior order of sainthood. A beatified person has the title of 'Blessed' before their name.

Some Roman Catholic churches in England are dedicated to saints who were killed because of their opposition to the Reformation, or have windows that commemorate beatified figures. Thomas More, Henry VIII's famous chancellor who was executed because of his opposition to the establishment of an English Church, is perhaps the best known of these post-Reformation saints.

Halos

It seems obvious that holy figures of various kinds are identified by halos – circles of bright light around their heads. But a halo, known also as a nimbus, is only one way by which these figures can be distinguished. Figures of Jesus, particularly when depicted as Christ in majesty (see page 178), are sometimes surrounded by a pointed oval form called a **mandorla** – known also as a *vesica piscis*, which means 'fish bladder' after its appearance. An **aureole** is a general background of a bright colour surrounding a person.

The decoration of a church

Symbols and signs

IN ADDITION to those objects associated with biblical characters, theologians and saints you will find considerable use made of other symbols that carry a special meaning. The most common of all is the cross, the symbol of Jesus' crucifixion but also of his resurrection. Perhaps its special role as the most important and most immediately recognizable of all Christian symbols is due to its being the most simple. The type of cross that has a long vertical post and a short horizontal one towards the top is called the Latin cross.

You will encounter different types of crosses. The Celtic cross, which you have already seen, has a ring that circles its head. A Greek cross has four arms of equal length. Other ones that you might encounter include the Maltese cross, with four equal arms that resemble darts pointing inwards; the patriarchal cross which has two horizontal bars, where the lower one is at the centre of the vertical post; and the cross of St Chad, named after the Northumbrian English saint, which takes the form of a solid square surrounded on four sides by T-shapes – itself a combination of two other early cross types called the potent cross and the quadrate cross. You can see St Chad's cross in abundance at the cathedral dedicated to him at Lichfield.

The familiar cross commonly takes several different forms.

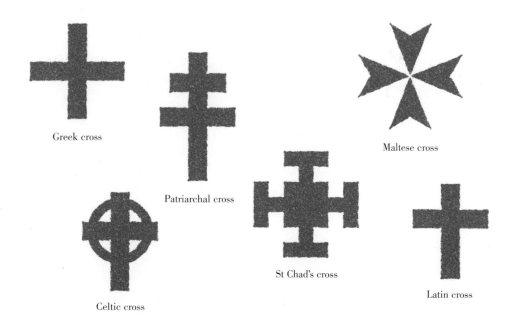

Greek cross

Patriarchal cross

Maltese cross

St Chad's cross

Celtic cross

Latin cross

The most splendid of all Victorian churches

St Giles' Roman Catholic Church, Cheadle, Staffordshire

THE VICTORIANS built many wonderful churches, and so the title of 'most splendid of all' cannot be awarded lightly. But it takes only a glance into the nave of St Giles to be persuaded that this is a building unlike any other.

The church was designed in 1841 by Augustus Pugin for the Earl of Shrewsbury, a leader of the Roman Catholic revival in England. Both men wanted a building that would be the ideal embodiment of the perfectly planned and richly decorated English church of the kind that might have existed everywhere if the Reformation had never happened. And so everything at St Giles is exactly as it should be: a steeple 61 m (200 ft) high; a fine south porch; a lady chapel; a chancel screen; an imposing 'doom' above the chancel arch; a chapel of the blessed sacrament; and a chancel fitted out as it would have been around the year 1400. You will find sedilia and a piscina laid out in a row, in mediaeval fashion, and facing them there is an Easter sepulchre. Astonishingly, this church survived the unsympathetic reordering processes of the 1960s.

Many architects were trying in the 1840s to build authentic gothic churches. What made Pugin special was his ability to design convincingly everything a building requires in a lively and creative mediaeval style. He covered the walls here with vivid floral patterns in red, gold and green, and designed all the metalwork, encaustic tiles, joinery and windows, as well as the vestments to be worn during services – and all in an entirely coherent style throughout. Furthermore, Pugin helped create a little gothic community just beyond the churchyard: he also designed the neighbouring former convent (with its recently excellently restored belfry) and the still-functioning school.

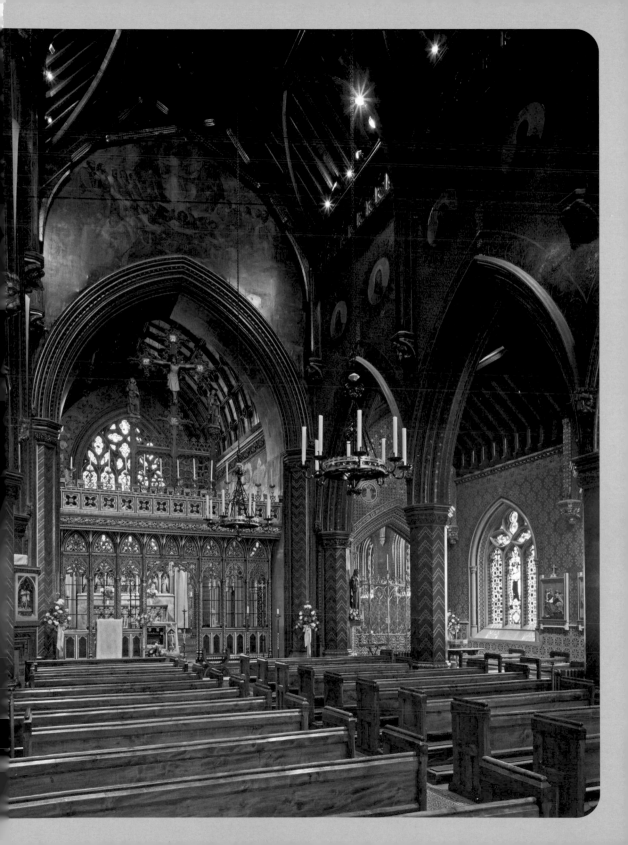

Other Christian symbols

The cross is not the only early symbol of Christianity. You may also find representations of fish in stylized form and these refer to Jesus' expression 'fishers of men' – and to the New Testament story of the feeding of five thousand people by the Sea of Galilee with only two fish. There are many other symbols that were regularly deployed by artists:

- The **lamb of God**. Lambs had significance as sacrificial animals in Jewish theology, and are referred to on several occasions in the New Testament. The first of these is when John the Baptist hails Jesus as the 'Lamb of God'. The phrase is repeated in the liturgy of holy communion, and is familiar too in its Latin form: *agnus dei*.
- The **dove**. Noah had sent a dove from the ark to see whether the waters of the flood had subsided; and the name Jonah means 'dove' in Hebrew. But the dove in Christian theology is a symbol of the Holy Spirit that descended on Jesus at his baptism by John, or on Jesus' disciples at the event commemorated by the festival of Pentecost.
- A **flame** also symbolizes the Holy Spirit.
- **Triangles** in various forms. Two of them superimposed, one facing up and one facing down, has long been the most commonly recognized symbol of Judaism, but a single triangle represents the Holy Trinity – the combination of God, God's son Jesus, and the Holy Spirit. It can also represent any of the many biblical phenomena that come in threes.

LEFT
Jesus carrying the lamb of God.

RIGHT
The Holy Spirit is usually represented by a dove.

Some of the finest stained glass ever made depicts flowers and plants. This beautiful example is at St Mary's, Brighton. Note the tree of knowledge depicted in the central panel.

- The **monogram** of Jesus, in various forms, including the initials INRI – the acronym of the Latin for 'Jesus of Nazareth, King of the Jews', the phrase written above Jesus' cross at his crucifixion. IHS is derived from Jesus' name in Latin letters, and IHC from the Greek version. XP and XPC are Latin approximations of the letters used in the Greek name and are less often encountered, although the former can be seen in the monogram called the labarum which juxtaposes the two letters.
- **Hands**, or **eyes**, to represent God.
- **Flowers** and **plants** of various kinds. **Vines**, recalled in many Old and New Testament stories, can often be seen: they represent both a rich harvest and the eucharist. Foliage can easily be turned into elegant repetitive patterns to form a backdrop to other more detailed symbols. Floral ornament could also be adapted for use in ironmongery, such as door handles or brass **coronas**.
- In Roman Catholic churches, the **sacred heart** with flames issuing from it or combined with a crown or a crown of thorns – a mystical symbol representing the love of Jesus for mankind.

Making stained glass

SURVIVING mediaeval stained glass – such as that at Canterbury cathedral, which dates from the late twelfth century – was made by assembling pieces of coloured glass into an iron frame using strips of lead to bind them together. By the early nineteenth century this skill had been largely lost, for artists were simply painting a design using enamel paint onto clear glass before firing in a kiln. The effect of this method can be seen in much post-Reformation glass: the colours tend to be washed out and brownish, and the naturalistic figures fail to make a visual impact.

In time the mediaeval methods were rediscovered and these are essentially those still used today. Using the artist's design a draughtsman prepares a cartoon – a full-scale drawing in black ink on a white background – and chooses suitable colours. Sheets of coloured glass are then selected, sometimes with irregularities of texture or streaks of colour that will enhance the final design. The glass is cut into pieces following the cartoon with the help of a grozing iron. Details of the design are painted onto the front surface of the glass; a wash of silver-stain or yellow-stain (made up from silver nitrate) can be applied to the back to create further variations in colour. Once fired in a kiln at a very high temperature, the pieces are assembled by slotting their edges into H-sectioned lead strips called calmes or cames. The finished panel is then sealed and attached to a frame so it can be fixed into a window aperture.

The Victorians rediscovered the art of creating stained glass that was as rich and vibrant as mediaeval examples had been.

Animals

SOME ANIMALS have specific biblical or Christian meanings; others are more playful or original representations by artists based on biblical stories and parables, or from non-Christian sources such as the signs of the zodiac or classical fables.

The decorative styles of gothic architecture provided limitless possibilities for a craftsman to portray living creatures.

- **The donkey** might be derived from the story of Balaam in the book of Numbers. Balaam's donkey stopped in its tracks when it saw an angel standing in the road to prevent Balaam from travelling against the wishes of God. This is a reminder that a humble creature may understand better than a man the will of God, and also a reference to the animal on which Jesus was to enter Jerusalem in the gospel of St Mark. On the other hand it might simply represent foolishness.

- **The monkey** is often seen in mediaeval carving, representing the bestial or perhaps simply comic nature of a creature so similar to a human being.

- **The eagle**, which we have seen representing the word of God flying down from the heavens as well as St John the Evangelist, was considered the most noble of birds by many civilizations.

You may remember from Chapter Two the delightful series of carvings of lively, comic scenes with animals in the Romanesque crypt of Canterbury cathedral (see page 64).

A rural masterpiece of the arts and crafts movement

All Saints, Brockhampton, Herefordshire

THE ARCHITECT William Lethaby, who was also well known as a theoretician and historian of architecture, designed very few buildings on his own before becoming a teacher but every one of them was a masterpiece. This small church, which was built from 1901–2, was commissioned by an American, Alice Foster, as a memorial to her parents, and it may have been the troublesome process of its construction that finally drove Lethaby away from practising as an architect. But what he created for posterity here is worth a hundred lesser buildings.

Lethaby believed deeply in the symbolic meaning of ancient styles of architecture, and that it was the architect's duty to be a craftsman who continually reinvents representational forms with his own hands. In common with others in the arts and crafts movement, he also believed that the careful design of the private home was the most important task in architecture. So All Saints' church has a domestic scale, and it comes as a surprise that its vaults, under the thatch, were actually cast in concrete. In fact the powerful atmosphere of the building results from the fusion of simple and massive forms with the delicacy of the detailing, designed by Lethaby himself or by his friends. The way in which the nave arches swoop down and blend into the walls, and the poignant contrasts between light and dark spaces, are unforgettable.

The decoration uses powerful symbolic or natural themes: in particular, the window tracery here is both unusual and beautiful, especially on the North transept where a small square window has an original knot-like pattern. When visiting the church be sure to look out for the smallest parts of the building, right down to the hinges on the front door which are in the form of plaits of iron. Few small buildings have the impact of this one.

Non-Christian imagery

SOME SYMBOLISM found in churches does not appear to be Christian at all, and may have found its way in as part of an attempt by Church authorities to assign to themselves robust pagan traditions that showed no signs of dying out.

Perhaps the best-known example is the green man, often just a face at the centre of a pattern of swirling greenery, who has a particular following among folklore enthusiasts. He appears sometimes in the august setting of a major cathedral and is thought to derive from Celtic mythology.

One of several striking images of a green man at Norwich cathedral.

Romanesque carvings can provide wonderful and sometimes quite shocking images. An example of the latter is the sheela-na-gig, a nude woman usually seen with her hands (or even her head) thrust indecently between her legs from behind. The finest set of Romanesque church carvings can be found on the exterior of the Norman church at Kilpeck in Herefordshire (see page 42). In Somerset there is a characteristic kind of squatting figure known as a hunky punk.

Outside a church you may find the familiar gargoyle: a carved caricature of a man, beast or monster, usually acting as a water spout or corbel. The word derives from an Old French word for a throat. As in the case of other non-Christian symbols outside a church, they seem to have been permitted to allow flamboyant and imaginative artists an opportunity to display their skills without getting in the way of the Christian messages within.

The decoration of a church

Heraldry

FOLLOWING the Reformation new types of decoration began to replace religious imagery. The parochial role of significant laypeople became more prominent at the expense of the church hierarchy or of the traditional objects of veneration, and as a result family heraldry began to be incorporated into stained-glass windows. In fact because heraldic symbolism is largely composed of simple shapes and distinct colours, it can be graphically powerful and has remained popular in modern design.

Heraldry is the art of family symbolism of the kind displayed on shields and banners. In England it is controlled by Garter King of Arms, whose permission must be sought before use. A coat of arms with a helmet or coronet and perhaps supporters is properly called an **achievement** and is designed according to strict rules and conventions using a mainly fixed series of colours and symbols that have picturesque Old French names.

The five basic colours used in traditional English heraldry are **azure** (blue), **gules** (red), **purpure** (purple), **sable** (black) and **vert** (green). To these are added the metals: **argent** (silver, which appears as white) and **or** (gold or yellow). A basic rule states that one colour cannot normally be placed directly on top of another, or one metal over another. An **escutcheon** or shield used for a man, or diamond-shaped **lozenge** for a woman, can be decorated or divided using a number of basic heraldic elements such as **furs**, patterns that imitate ermine. Other common terms include **chevrons**, shaped like arrowheads, and **bends**, which are diagonal bands. Smaller chevrons and bends are called **chevronels** and **bendlets**. **Abatements** are decorative marks denoting illegitimacy. Other common terms include the **orle**, an outline of a shield; the **tressure**, which is a narrow orle; and the **saltire**, which is an X-shaped cross. The royal arms of England are described by heralds as being 'Gules, three lions passant guardant Or', and of Scotland as 'Or, a lion rampant gules armed and langued azure, within a double tressure flory counter-flory Gules'.

An important feature of a family achievement is that it will change in a largely pre-determined way across the generations according to the status of the holders and the families that they marry into. By tracing these changes it is possible to follow how families intermarry.

The familiar royal arms have varied throughout history: until 1801 they included three lilies, called fleurs-de-lys, to signify a claim to the French throne. Some heraldic symbols denote the holding of ecclesiastical office. A stylized pallium – a white band originally worn by bishops across the shoulders – signifies the archbishop of Canterbury.

Non-figurative decoration

PROTESTANT reformers were anxious to rid churches of anything that either appeared superstitious or might divert worshippers from listening to their preacher. That did not mean, however, that all decoration was banned; it simply took on a different form.

The most common form of the new decoration was a painted wall panel that listed the ten commandments transcribed by Moses and which appear in the Bible in the books of Exodus and Deuteronomy. When churches were restored in the nineteenth century these often rather dour tables largely disappeared; the place to see them now is in seventeenth- or eighteenth-century churches that have been restored, such as in Christopher Wren's City churches in London. Painted texts in general, usually quoting biblical sayings, were used right up to the nineteenth century as a way of decorating walls that would not be theologically problematic.

Heraldry

A statute of King Charles II in 1660 required that the arms of the monarch should henceforth be displayed in all churches, and you may also find examples of royal arms from before this time that have survived to this day. Many churches have continued the practice, and indeed some have commissioned new ones.

The introduction of heraldry into a church was, however, by no means a Protestant invention. The strong connection between patron families and their churches had always meant that a family shield was likely to be displayed prominently, particularly on tombs. You might also come across a hatchment – a diamond-shaped panel displaying a coat of arms against a black background. These were made for the funeral processions of the nobility and gentry, and sometimes remained in the church as a memorial long after the interment.

The emblem of King Edmund, from a window in the church near his presumed martyrdom site at Hoxne in Suffolk.

Finding iconography in a church

THE NUMBER of places where iconographic decoration can be found in a church is almost endless.

- **On the walls**. Mediaeval churches were often decorated from head to foot with painted images, linked by colourful floral patterns. A few of these have survived, at least partially. Some Victorian churches revived the art of wall painting and stencilling.

- **Stained-glass windows**. At Fairford in Gloucestershire you can find an almost complete set of pre-Reformation stained glass; it includes scenes representative of just about all the major themes listed in this chapter. Another famous set is at St Neot in Cornwall. Perhaps it is the stained glass of the Victorian era that more than anything else arouses strong opinions among visitors to churches today. The rediscovery of the original methods and a great deal of experimentation (see page 196) resulted in the design of complete iconographic schemes across the windows of churches. It was in the windows, too, that latter-day benefactors often wanted to be commemorated or to establish memorials to members of their families. When fashion turned against the powerful colours of these windows, a great many were taken out or subjected to a humiliating treatment usually called pickling – the eradication of background colour, leaving the figures floating in a sea of clear glass. On the other hand, the sometimes stark design of modern churches was often balanced by the rich colours of strong abstract designs. In recent times figurative treatment has returned. In Durham cathedral a window that celebrates the millennium includes images of mining equipment and even of a computer screen. The artist, Joseph Nuttgens, is himself the grandson of one of the masters of twentieth-century glass.

- **Sculpture groups**. Sculpture is more expensive than stained glass, and so complete iconographic groups are rare outside the major churches and cathedrals, where they have made something of a comeback recently. A good example is the series of modern martyrs recently installed at the West front of Westminster Abbey. Again, the Victorians provided some magnificent precedents. At the Anglican cathedral at Cork in the Republic of Ireland the architect William Burges was given a rare opportunity to imitate the work of the great mediaeval masons and install a complete iconographical scheme that includes a panel illustrating the resurrection; rows of wise and foolish virgins from a New Testament parable; and the traditional portrayal of opposing images representing 'church' and 'synagogue'.

- **Pulpits and fonts**. Looking at the panels around the bases of pulpits and fonts you can often find carved scenes, some very old. The earliest designs are Saxon and are characterized by floral patterns. Victorian architects again imitated mediaeval precedent by constructing some stupendous and highly ornamental timber font covers many metres high. Pulpits typically had images of famous biblical preachers or scenes from Jesus' work as a teacher around their bases. Some Victorian ones have wonderful geometrical patterns in ornamental stones and marbles.

- In the **roof**. You have already encountered images of angels in the design of the magnificent roofs of East Anglian wool churches.

The fourteenth-century wall painting of the murder of Thomas à Becket, at the remarkable parish church at Brookland in Kent.

Numbers

SOME NUMBERS have special importance in Christian theology, and they often reoccur in church iconography. The most important of these include:

3   the Holy Trinity: God, Jesus and the Holy Spirit. A triangle is a symbol that illustrates the indivisibility of these three central aspects of the Christian deity

4   represents the evangelists and their gospels

7   is a number that has particular significance in Judaism, in particular because it represents the number of days in the week: the six days of creation together with the day of rest

10   is the number of commandments that Moses received from God

12   is the number that can refer to the 12 tribes of Israel and to their New Testament counterpart: the 12 apostles of Jesus.

Moses holding the tablets inscribed with the ten commandments.

Everything together

MANY OF THE most impressive churches of all derive their power from the sheer cumulative effect of all the iconography contained within them.

Some of the most memorable churches of this kind were built during the Art Nouveau period of design at the end of the nineteenth and beginning of the twentieth century when the political and religious power of the Church of England was arguably at its peak. The best-known example is the church of Holy Trinity in Sloane Avenue, London, which was designed by John Dando Sedding and Henry Wilson with contributions from many artist friends. Although the design was not in the end carried out in full, the effect is distinctly theatrical.

There are several others which are equally powerful. St Bartholomew's in Brighton, also designed by Wilson, is an example, and so is the very fine church of St Andrew, at Roker near Sunderland, by Edward Prior. These structures do not, however, need to be large to be effective. The little church of the 1890s dedicated most unusually to the Wisdom of God, at Lower Kingswood in Surrey, resplendent with mosaics and coloured stone, is one example, as is St Martin's, Blackheath, from the same period.

The use of incense as an inducement to prayer and spirituality, rare in the Church of England and disapproved of in some circles, can add a further dimension to the experience of churchgoing.

A circular window in the form of a decorative wheel is called a rose window. It can be one of the most powerful elements of church design.

CHAPTER SIX

Churches worldwide

THE VILLAGE church and the great cathedrals of the cities are a major feature of predominantly Christian countries worldwide. In each land you will come across different architectural characteristics, but you will also find much in common with the churches you know from home. You will also discover that, just as in England, a church has much to tell about local history and design traditions.

LEFT The birth of Jesus, depicted at St Julian's, Kingston Buci, West Sussex.

The first churches

THE HISTORICAL origins of church building are important because they established some of the basic ideas about what a structure devised for Christian worship should look like.

For most of the first four centuries after the death of Jesus, Christians were a small persecuted sect and citizens of an otherwise pagan Roman Empire. They are likely to have congregated in private houses or in small buildings. By the beginning of the third century, however, they needed to celebrate the eucharist in a room large enough to allow a proper distinction between the clergy and a communion table on the one hand, and the congregation on the other; in addition, minor spaces were allocated for baptism and for those who were not yet communing members of the church. Various storage rooms were also necessary. A number of these small complexes dating from this early period have been discovered across the territories of the Empire.

The great change came when the Emperor Constantine, who ruled from AD 306–337, announced that Christianity would be recognized as an official religion. This came in his Edict of Milan of 313, and from then onwards he personally promoted the building of new churches across his realm. The result was that Christianity had for the first time a public face, and it needed imposing new buildings in which to display it.

The church of St John Lateran in Rome has been rebuilt many times but its basic form is similar to that of the original fourth-century building.

Churches worldwide

The first churches as we know them date from this era. Constantine promoted the building of St John Lateran in Rome, originally constructed around the year 320. Although completely rebuilt several times the form of the church today is similar to that of the original structure. It takes the form of a basilica – a broad and long nave, separated by a colonnade from aisles on either side. In fact here, as in other early churches, each aisle was divided into two longways by a further colonnade. Above the aisles a row of clerestory windows let light into the nave. There was an apse at the Eastern end as well as symmetrical projections to the North and South for storing offerings. The building was large enough to accommodate several thousand worshippers. Across the Empire, remains can be found of several Constantinian churches which were built like this.

Constantine was responsible for two other buildings which have also come to influence the design of churches ever since. One was the parent church of the whole of the Western Church: St Peter's in Rome, which was complete and partly decorated by the time of the emperor's death in 337. This first building is long demolished, but accurate views of it were drawn by artists around the time the present cathedral went up in the sixteenth and seventeenth centuries.

Old St Peter's was a basilica-type church, like St John Lateran, and was built directly above an old Christian cemetery and the shrine of St Peter himself. It did, however, include one important innovation: transepts. The high altar was located above the shrine (in fact, at the geographical western end of the building) and at

The Anastasis Rotunda in the church of the Holy Sepulchre in Jerusalem was built around the supposed site of Jesus' tomb.

The former church of Hagia Sophia in Istanbul, today the Ayasofya Museum, was built in the mid-sixth century by the Emperor Justinian.

each side of it there were large wings that could accommodate either the clergy during services or pilgrims who came to see the shrine. It was thus the predecessor of the large transepts built in mediaeval cathedrals to permit a flow of visitors and to maximize the opportunities for side altars.

The third of the three great Constantinian churches has also been largely rebuilt but in a way that captures its original character. In some respects it is the most remarkable. This is the part of the Church of the Holy Sepulchre in the old walled city of Jerusalem that is properly known as the Anastasis Rotunda.

Constantine's mother, Helena, was a devout Christian and she devoted her life to the discovery of sites and relics from the life of Jesus. The emperor was the first to commemorate these with new churches. The location of Jesus' tomb was a few metres from the site of the crucifixion itself, and a large complex went up to house both of them. One major structure was a basilica church which has since been replaced by a largely twelfth-century church, but the much rebuilt rotunda, a tall building on a circular plan, can still be seen. The tomb is located at the centre of it. Small versions of the rotunda were built on other holy sites in the region.

Centralized churches

In fact the centralized building under a great dome subsequently became one of the dominant forms for churches particularly in Eastern Europe and around Constantinople, the capital of the Roman Empire from 330. Around the Balkans and present-day Greece and Turkey a new type of building technology developed that allowed a dome to be built up by bridging the corners of stone rooms with curved triangular stretches of masonry called pendentives. The characteristic style that emerged alongside this discovery is called Byzantine architecture, and you can recognize

Churches worldwide

it by its proliferation of domes – usually flattish, like saucers and unlike tall Roman domes – and arcades. The most splendid of these buildings were decorated with golden mosaics: these combine with the strong daylight filtering in through the small windows punched through thick walls to create a rich and startling effect.

The most famous of all these Byzantine churches is the former church of Hagia Sofia in Istanbul, as Constantinople is now called. It was originally built from 532–7 by Justinian, emperor of what was by then a separate Eastern Roman Empire. The church consists of one vast space dominated by a saucer dome; this great dome is flanked by a pair of large half-domes to the West and East, and smaller half-domes seem to cascade around the edges of the building. When the building was a church – it subsequently became a mosque and museum – it was awash with golden mosaics and symbolic decorations. Side areas were divided from the main space with beautifully carved arcades. Small centralized churches with complex geometries went up right across Justinian's empire. One of the most delightful is St Vitale at the Italian city of Ravenna with its magnificent mosaics.

The Eastern Orthodox Church

The national Churches of Russia and some East European countries form together the Eastern Orthodox Church, and they have traditionally always been built in the Byzantine style. The interiors of their churches are heavily decorated with icons and, where possible, golden mosaics. The other distinct difference between the interior of an Eastern Orthodox church and a Western one is the substantial screen, called an iconostasis, that separates the Eastern end of the church from the nave.

The iconostasis, a substantial screen decorated with icons, is a characteristic feature of an Eastern Orthodox church.

The people's brutalism: a new architecture for a new way of worship

St Paul, Bow Common, London

DESIGNING A CHURCH presents an architect with an unusual opportunity to try out abstract ideas, because it is a building that requires a large mystical space with very little in the way of practicalities beyond a good roof and solid walls. For that reason churches often represent the latest in experimental thinking, even at times when churchgoing in general may be on the decline.

The church of St Paul, at Bow Common in East London, created a sensation when it was opened in 1960 because of the bold way it combined the current fashion for gritty 'brutalist' architecture with a popular movement that stressed the communality of worship. The architects, Robert Maguire and Keith Murray, founded the New Churches Research Group, an organization which aimed to create an inspirational architecture that suited progressive liturgical ideas and in particular a revived bond between priest and people. The church at Bow consists of a single space centred on a lively and canopied concrete altar sitting on a predella; the great glazed lantern overhead and the austere nature of the other fittings reinforce rather than distract from the act of communal worship. It is interesting to note that Robert Maguire described himself as a 'rebellious' Roman Catholic, whereas Keith Murray was a High Church Anglican; the vicar – Gresham Kirkby – was a Marxist.

The late 1950s and 1960s were a fruitful time for a new generation of artists and designers. St Paul's introduced the work of graphic designer Ralph Beyer to a wide and appreciative audience: he designed here the dramatic lettering, announcing 'the gate of heaven', around the porch. The murals that decorate the triangular spandrels between the central nave and the aisle were designed by Charles Lutyens, a great-nephew of the architect Sir Edwin Lutyens.

Reusing historical ideas

Architects have often wanted to recapture the basic layout and atmosphere of these famous old churches because they have become symbolic of the oldest values of Christianity. Even today when a parish church is being refurbished, the idea of reverting to a simple, perhaps whitewashed, space with a few good fittings often seems a powerful one to the incumbent and congregation, even if in fact it does not particularly well suit a Victorian church that was originally designed to be loaded with symbolic art and furniture.

Nearly every church derives something from these early buildings. Of course the typical basilica church, with nave and aisles, owes a great deal to its Roman forbearers. Others make more specific references. In the twelfth century the Order of the Knights Templar built tiny reproductions of the Jerusalem rotunda as a celebration perhaps of their exploits in the Holy Land: the most famous has become the Temple Church in London, although there are at least three other surviving round churches in England (see page 60). The best of these can be found, heavily restored, in Cambridge.

Towards the end of the nineteenth century and into the twentieth many of the different Western Christian Churches began to rethink some of their ideas about how their buildings should look, possibly because of a feeling of suffocation from the intense nature of High Victorian design. One result was a revival of Byzantine architecture which had in fact made intermittent reappearances in Western Europe since the 1820s. In the 1890s Cardinal Vaughan, leader of the Roman Catholic Church in England, decided to build his new cathedral in what he called a 'primitive' form of Christian architecture. The result, Westminster cathedral, designed by John F. Bentley, is the most magnificent Byzantine building in Britain. A further advantage of the choice of style was that it did not seem to rival the gothic, Protestant, Westminster Abbey which was close by.

The early twentieth-century architect and designer Ninian Comper, whose work can be seen in parish churches right across England, was an enthusiast for the revival of very early church forms. His whitewashed spaces, set off by ornate and delicate gilded metalwork, sometimes have a Mediterranean feel to them. One of his trademarks was a curtained ciborium or canopy over the altar – something that we know existed at Constantine's church of St Peter in Rome. Comper also liked to bring his communion tables out Westwards towards the congregations. This was controversial at the time but ironically became a forerunner for today's fashion for a centralized worship space.

The most interesting churches in the region today are actually comparatively modern, built mainly by Franciscan or Benedictine orders, and functioning in part as modern shrines for pilgrims.

- **The Church of the Multiplication of Loaves and Fishes, Tabgha**
  This church, designed by Anton Goergen and Fritz Baumann for the adjacent German Benedictine monastery and consecrated in 1982, is the latest in a series of buildings erected on the site to commemorate the miracle of the loaves and fishes by the Sea of Galilee (see page 180). The design of the building with its colonnaded narthex (portico or lobby), courtyard and basilica is closely based on that of the early sixth-century Byzantine predecessor on the site. Traces of the wonderful mosaic floor of the older building depicting the loaves and fishes can still be seen incorporated into the new building.

  Close to this building is the tiny **Sanctuary of the Primacy of St Peter**, which stands on the very edges of the sea alongside steps carved into the rock on which Jesus was said to have walked. It was built by Franciscans in 1933–4.
- **The Shrine of the Beatitudes**
  The Italian architect Antonio Barlozzi built several very fine buildings on biblical sites in a style which mixed traditional Byzantine forms with idiosyncratic and sometimes expressionist detailing. This shrine, which is a domed, octagonal church, sits on a hill top above the Sea of Galilee and was built in 1936. It commemorates the Sermon on the Mount (see page 179). Barlozzi also designed:
- **The Church of the Transfiguration** atop Mount Tabor, to commemorate the scene described in the gospel of Matthew, 17, where Jesus appeared before his disciples as a divine being, conversing with Moses and Elijah. The building was designed in a rich, ornamental Roman style and built in 1921–5.
- **Dominus Flevit**
  Barlozzi's curious little structure of 1955 is designed in the shape of a teardrop to commemorate the site in Jerusalem where, according to Luke, 19, 'Jesus wept' in prophesying the future destruction of the city.
- **The Church of the Annunciation, Nazareth**
  The largest Christian basilica in the Middle East, this church was built by the Italian architect Giovanni Muzio on the site of earlier buildings and completed in 1969. Its lower level incorporates the cave that functioned as a church in Byzantine times.

Churches in the Holy Land

THE PLACES where Jesus lived and worked during his lifetime, which are located in present-day Israel and Palestine, have ironically found themselves on the edges of organized Christianity for most of its existence. It was not until the reign of Constantine, the first Christian Roman Emperor, that the various sites mentioned in the New Testament were converted into holy places with permanent buildings. With the exception of the Church of the Nativity in Bethlehem and some of the earliest surviving parts of the Church of the Holy Sepulchre in Jerusalem, these were modest structures which have almost entirely disappeared or been hidden by subsequent rebuilding.

The Shrine of the Beatitudes in the Galilee is one of a series of remarkable buildings designed for the Franciscan order in Israel.

National families of churches

FOR ALL THEIR similarities, the churches in different parts of the world have their own familiar characteristics. In some places these are quite distinct. Here are some of the best known:

Norway

One of the unique architectural treasures of the country is its collection of mediaeval stave churches. Timber churches were once common in many European countries, and in Norway itself there may have been as many as 2,000. Only 28 survive today. One of the finest, at Urnes right in the centre of the country, was built soon after 1130 and is included in UNESCO's World Heritage List.

The churches were mainly erected in the twelfth and thirteenth centuries and are constructed from pine. Both inside and out they are entirely built and clad in timber; the larger ones have bold, simple wooden columns inside. Their steep roofs are covered in shingles and have tall spires. Some of their decoration, for example the carved panels of plants and birds at Urnes, date from the period of their original building, but many of them have intricate painted interiors dating from the post-Reformation era.

The stave church is an important part of the Norwegian national architectural heritage. This one, at Lom, was mainly built around the middle of the twelfth century.

Germany

Modern Germany was created in the nineteenth century by amalgamating a number of smaller states, but there are some architectural characteristics that can be seen right across the country. The most distinct of these is perhaps the hall church. This is a type of building that differs from the familiar basilica because the aisles rise up to the height of the nave.

Most of the best known of these churches can be found in the centre and north of the country. The first and one of the best examples of a gothic hall church is St Elizabeth, Marburg, where the nave was under construction in the mid-thirteenth century. Another fine hall church is the cathedral at Minden, the nave of which was built slightly later. The external appearance of a hall church is quite different from the basilica model because of the absence of aisle roofs and clerestory windows, and the interiors are characteristically airy.

Around Rostock and Lübeck, the cities of the Baltic coast, you can find impressive churches built in the Backstein style. The word means 'brick', and even the largest buildings were constructed with it because of the absence of stone in these areas. Ornament and colour were introduced through variations in the types of brick used.

The hall church, where the aisles are the same height as the nave, is a characteristic of much German late mediaeval architecture.

Flamboyant tracery is carved in a form reminiscent of flames. This example is one of many from the city of Rouen in Normandy.

Some of the most astonishing of all gothic church interiors can be found in Saxony. Here the skill of ornamental stone vaulting was developed to an unparalleled degree. Stone ribs twist and turn like tendrils across the roofs of churches. One of the most spectacular can be found at the church of St Anne at Annaburg, built at the beginning of the sixteenth century. At Ingolstadt in Bavaria the parish church has a remarkable openwork carving on the vault of a nave chapel of a type called 'thorny rib work', and resembling a knot of branches

France

France was the birthplace of the gothic style and has a great richness of church architecture of all kinds. It does, however, have some decorative forms that seem distinctly French.

Perhaps the best known of these is the flamboyant style, a particularly rich variety of late gothic architecture where mouldings such as window tracery are carved into flame-like shapes. In Rouen along the River Seine in Normandy there are several examples, especially at the large church of St Maclou in the centre of the city. Churches with flamboyant details can be found all over the country. In Paris, Saint-Séverin, a large parish church on the Left Bank, is considered to be one of the finest examples.

Another particularly French style is called rayonnant or 'radiant', characterized by the wheel-like designs of rose windows.

Czech Republic

A style of vaulting developed in the churches and houses of Bohemia (today's Czech Republic and areas of the surrounding countries) that was quite unlike the type of church ceiling seen elsewhere. This is called the diamond vault, and it resembles a sheet of folded paper without ribs. Fine examples can be found in the monastery of Bechyně and at Tábor and Soběslav, three towns in close proximity to each other to the south of Prague. Further examples of diamond, or 'cell', vaults can be found in northern Poland, in Hungary and in the German region of Saxony, where they originally came from. Although mainly designed in the early sixteenth century, these remarkable roofs look as if they belong to the experimental architecture of the early twentieth century.

Diamond vaults resemble folded paper. They were mainly built in today's Czech Republic and Poland in the early sixteenth century.

Modern church architects

DESIGNING churches continues to be an exciting and demanding task, and in recent years there has been something of a revival of interest in what is again being seen as a prestigious aspect of the architect's work. Some well-known architects have revitalized their careers thanks to the design of a new church that has joined the canon of influential buildings worldwide.

- **Peter Zumthor** is one of Switzerland's best-known architects today, and he has become world famous for the somewhat mystical stone-clad thermal baths he designed at Vals in the east of the country. He first made his name with a tiny chapel at Somvix, some 15 miles away across the mountains. This elegant building is constructed of timber and designed with a plan in the form of a teardrop.

- **Mario Botta** is another Swiss architect, and he rose to prominence in the 1970s as a villa designer in the Italian-speaking Ticino region. He has since designed several influential churches that deploy his characteristic bold geometry. His building at Evry, south of Paris, takes the form of a tall, pink brick cylinder; its oblique roof is planted with trees. At its completion in 1995 it became the first new cathedral to be built in France since the 1789 revolution.

- **Renzo Piano**, the Italian who leapt to fame as the co-architect with Richard Rogers of the Pompidou Centre in Paris in the early 1970s, completed thirty years later a very different type of building: a vast but low church on a spiral plan that perhaps resembles a tortoise. The complex includes an external concourse that can accommodate 30,000 pilgrims near the shrine of Padre Pio at San Giovanni Rotondo in Puglia in south-east Italy.

- **Richard Meier** is an American architect famed for his austere white buildings. He won a prestigious international competition in 1996 to design a new church in Rome for the millennium celebrations and the silver jubilee of Pope John Paul II. The building, completed in 2003, occupies a prominent triangular site in the Tor Tre Teste area and is formed from three tall, arching shells with large areas of glazing in between.

Evry Cathedral near Paris was designed by the Swiss architect Mario Botta using his characteristic simple, bold geometry and high quality brickwork.

• British architect **John Pawson** is similarly renowned for his ascetic, minimalist design. In 1999 he was commissioned to design new monastic buildings at Nový Dvůr in the Czech Republic – a choice that seemed surprising at the time since he was perhaps best known as the architect of small luxurious homes, and shops such as the Calvin Klein stores in New York and Tokyo. But his highly disciplined approach has transferred powerfully to religious buildings.

• **Tadao Ando**, the Japanese architect, is considered a master of elegant concrete design; one of his most remarkable buildings is his 1989 Church of the Light at Ibaraki-shi in the Osaka prefecture. The East wall of the church consists of a bare panel of concrete pierced from side to side and top to bottom by a cross of daylight. His compatriot **Shigeru Ban** designed a paper church at Kobe in 1995.

Churches and architectural history

YOU HAVE SEEN throughout this book that churches are very often impressive buildings. As a result, they have a special place in the history of architecture in general.

Some architects first made their name by winning competitions for designs for new churches. Others used church building as an opportunity to experiment with new ideas. Perhaps it is the fact that a church is a relatively large building for a small number of particular symbolic functions that makes its design so interesting to architects. There is plenty of space for the designer to 'play with', and they are often prestigious buildings which enjoy a relatively large budget. They can also provide a rare opportunity for designers to create a sense of mystery and surprise in design which cannot easily be expressed in other ways. In addition, churches also need to convey power and hierarchy, and they often are intended to encapsulate some traces of both architectural and religious history.

For all these reasons there are some churches that have a special part to play in the history of architecture. Getting to know them well is a way of becoming familiar with

The Grundtvig Church in northern Copenhagen was designed by Peder Vilhelm Jensen Klint. It commemorates N.F.S. Grundtvig, the great Danish theologian and educator.

some of the leading themes in European culture. The fact that many twentieth-century ones were built at times of religious doubt, for example after the devastations of two world wars, seems further to add to the atmosphere of intrigue that they can inspire.

The following are particularly important to architectural history:

Grundtvig Church, Copenhagen, Denmark, 1913–40

Building what was to become one of the largest projects in Scandinavia was so lengthy an undertaking that it took three generations of an architectural family – Peder Vilhelm Jensen Klint, Kaare Klint and Esben Klint – to complete it. Intended as a memorial to Denmark's greatest educator, this massive church is particularly significant for the way in which it transformed a modest gothic brick-building tradition into an expressive modern work. The Western tower is based on the typical form of a Danish village church magnified many times over.

Nôtre Dame, Le Raincy, France, 1922–3

The church of Nôtre Dame at Le Raincy just east of Paris is an important Modernist structure. It was designed by Auguste Perret in 1922.

This church, designed by Auguste Perret, was a revolutionary structure entirely constructed from concrete. The walls are studded from top to bottom with coloured glass to create a shimmering, warm space which is scarcely interrupted by the slender columns that support the shallow curved vault. This is the place to visit for anyone who is convinced that concrete can only be a cold, unfriendly material.

The English Church abroad

THE CHURCH of England built churches abroad for its expatriate members and for diplomatic communities in capital cities. Some of these buildings were designed by leading London architects and they often resemble the type of church they would have designed for a site in England. The Anglican church of St Alban's in Copenhagen, for example, was designed in 1885 by Arthur Blomfield, a prolific Victorian church designer, and it brings a touch of the English village green to its pastoral setting on the edge of the historic city centre. St James' cathedral in Jerusalem, by James Johns and Matthew Habershon, is a similarly surprising sight.

Perhaps the most distinguished of these architects was George Edmund Street, the designer of the Law Courts in the Strand in London. In 1856 he won a competition to design the Crimea Memorial Church in Istanbul. Street also built for the Church of England in Rome and Genoa, and at Mürren in Switzerland.

Leading English architects also designed for the Anglican Churches of other countries. Street himself built for American Episcopalians in Rome and Paris. G.F. Bodley designed Washington National Cathedral: the foundation stone was laid in 1907 but the impressive gothic building was not completed until 1990. J.L. Pearson, the architect of Truro cathedral, also designed St John's cathedral in Brisbane, the capital of the Australian state of Queensland. In Melbourne the Roman Catholic cathedral was designed by William Wardell, a recent immigrant from England; the Anglican one was originally designed by Englishman William Butterfield, as was the cathedral at Adelaide.

Washington National Cathedral, a major building of the Episcopal Church in the United States of America, was designed by the British architect G.F. Bodley.

Church of the Sacred Heart, Vinohrady, Prague, Czech Republic, 1928–32

Slovenian architect Jože Plečnik developed an idiosyncratic interpretation of the neo-classical style. This is the Church of the Sacred Heart at Vinohrady, Prague.

The Slovenian-born architect Jože Plečnik produced some of the most extraordinary buildings of the century, mainly in a very idiosyncratic neo-classical style with odd distended proportions and curious detailing. This church was originally designed while he was working for Tomás Masaryk, the first president of the newly established republic of Czechoslovakia. The building is in dark brick studded with stone to give the impression of ermine, but its most striking feature is the tall Eastern tower which is as wide as the church at its base but strangely shallow. A long ramp leads all the way up through it, passing a pair of gigantic, facing transparent clock faces.

Modern churches around the world

ARCHITECTS TODAY build churches across the world that continue to express the limitless ways in which traditional rituals can be celebrated, sometimes using sophisticated constructional techniques but occasionally relying on enthusiastic local labour. In every continent you can find remarkable new churches. Recent ones which have attracted international attention include:

- **Urubo, Bolivia**: architect Jae Cha designed a strikingly simple round church from timber, clad with corrugated translucent polycarbonate panels, for a village near Santa Cruz in the central part of the country. The church was built by the villagers themselves.
- Another recent South American building to have impressed critics worldwide is a new chapel for Los Nogales school at **Bogotá**, the capital of **Colombia**. The whole of the north-west wall of the chapel opens out in the form of a pair of massive timber doors to create an external worship space.
- In **Alabama, USA**, an architectural practice called Rural Studio combines the energies of architects, teachers, students and villagers to create remarkable structures from local and recycled materials in poor communities. In 2002 they completed the **Antioch Baptist Church** in Perry County.
- In the same year Mathew & Ghosh Architects completed a sophisticated sparkling white church with an auditorium plan at **Bangalore** in **India**.
- Ciel Rouge Création, a partnership which combines the talents of French architect Henri Gueydan and Japanese designer Fumiko Kaneko, created a church at **Harajyuku** in **Tokyo** that was opened in 2005. Its interior takes the form of a cascade of sweeping white arches.

Bethel Baptist church at Bangalore, India, designed by Mathew & Gosh.

Nôtre Dame-du-Haut, Ronchamp, France, 1950–5

Le Corbusier's pilgrimage church at Ronchamp, in the east of France, is one of the most important monuments of post-Second World War architecture.

Le Corbusier is often considered to have been the most influential architect of the twentieth century, and his religious projects rank as some of his most important work. This one is a small pilgrimage chapel built on a historic sacred site whose previous church had been destroyed during the Second World War. Like a vast concrete sculpture that has been compared to a ship or even a nuns' wimple, this building with its thick punctured walls, its mysteriously lit internal space and its rolling roof forms is undoubtedly the most famous church of its era.

Churches worldwide

St Mark, Bjorkhagen, Stockholm, Sweden, 1956–60

The Swedish architect Sigurd Lewerentz, like Jože Plečnik before him, has the reputation of a mystic, and his churches are similarly unforgettable but slightly unsettling. This one was among his final projects, designed when he was in his mid-70s, and is located in an outer suburb of Stockholm. Lewerentz revered the humble brick and the distinct character of the church, including its vault, is created by exploiting this most simple of forms often through gentle curves and unexpected openings. The austere furnishings and the sparkling lamps create an atmosphere that has a primitive quality to it. Some years later Lewerentz built a similar church at Klippan on the south-west coast of Sweden.

St Bride, East Kilbride, Great Britain, 1963–5

From the mid-1950s the established Glasgow practice of Gillespie, Kidd & Coia was actually led by architects Isi Metzstein and Andy MacMillan, and they designed a number of striking Roman Catholic churches and other religious buildings, particularly in the Scottish New Towns. The church of St Bride is an outstanding example, although it soon lost its tall brick campanile following structural problems. The church itself takes the form of a large, austere brick hall, reminiscent of a fortress, with unusual indirect lighting through angled wall openings. Its simple open plan was intended to suit the requirements of 'Vatican II'.

St Bride, in the Scottish new town of East Kilbride, attracted international attention on its completion in 1965. The architects were Gillespie, Kidd & Coia.

Cathedral of the Virgin Mary, Neviges, Germany, 1964–72

German architect Gottfried Böhm is the son of Dominikus Böhm, a distinguished church architect of the first half of the century. At Neviges, a small town in the Rheinland near Wuppertal, he designed a pilgrimage church as well as a colonnaded route through the town leading up to it. The whole building is made from cast concrete, its craggy overall form suggesting a mountain or a tent – both images related to the idea of pilgrimage as an ordeal and an ascent. The sculptural interior is equally dramatic.

Chapel, Brion Vega Cemetery, San Vito d'Altivole, Italy, 1978

The Brion Vega cemetery chapel by Carlo Scarpa at San Vito d'Altivole in north-west Italy is both evocative and subtle.

Carlo Scarpa was renowned for his skill at creating poignant spaces with sculptural concrete forms, particularly when designing new interiors for old buildings. He designed a private cemetery at a village north-west of Venice in the early 1970s, eventually adding this small bunker-like building in the corner of it in the last year of his life. A careful look, however, will reveal a structure of great subtlety and delicacy that has the character of an ancient tomb.

Churches and synagogues

THE ARCHITECTURE of churches might not seem to have much in common with that of a synagogue designed for the very different practices of Judaism. In fact there are some interesting points of comparison, and ones which suggest that church design demonstrates universal values that can be seen right across the Western world.

The focal point in every synagogue is the niche on the Eastern wall, which is called the ark. This is the place for the scrolls of the law – rolls of parchment inscribed by hand with the text in Hebrew of the first five books of the Bible and clad in a velvet or metal casing. A lamp hangs in front of the ark, and at either side of it there are seats for the rabbi and important visitors. At the centre of the hall and in the middle of the congregation is a platform, called a *bimah*, for readings and prayers. A traditional orthodox synagogue will have an upper gallery where women can sit apart from the men below.

It can thus be seen that the basic arrangement is similar to that of an evangelical church. In fact, because of the minority (and persecuted) status of Jews for many centuries, European synagogue architecture really only began to develop in the late seventeenth century and it closely parallels that of religious dissenters such as Puritans and Quakers. The Great Synagogue in Amsterdam of 1671 became a prototype, particularly for the first one built in England, at Bevis Marks in London, of 1699.

A synagogue is planned around a central platform called a *bimah*. In some respects the layout resembles that of evangelical churches.

Building a modern cathedral

BUILDING a cathedral today is as exciting an experience as it ever was, and the opportunity still exists to create a rich and varied building which is capable of inspiring devotion and awe.

In 1996 the Roman Catholic diocese of Los Angeles held a competition to replace its mainly late nineteenth-century cathedral of St Vibiana which had been damaged in the earthquake of 1994. The city, like many others in the United States, has a very rich heritage of church buildings designed for many different Christian denominations, including not only Roman Catholics and various international Protestant organizations but also the Eastern and Russian Orthodox Churches and some local communities. These buildings have been designed over the last hundred years in a wide variety of styles, including most European ones and also some interesting Californian varieties such as Spanish Colonial mixed with Art Deco. There is even a Danish Lutheran church with a characteristic stepped Western gable. In addition to housing regular services, some have been intended to provide a rich backdrop to public events – including, for example, the Good Shepherd Catholic church in Beverley Hills, a favoured venue for glamorous Hollywood weddings. In some of these churches the quality of the interior fittings is, by European standards, stupendous.

Consequently, expectations were high for the new building in Los Angeles, which was to be located on an elevated site a little way to the north of the old cathedral. The competition was won by the distinguished Spanish architect Rafael Moneo, and his new Cathedral of Our Lady of the Angels was opened in 2002.

The cathedral is a spectacular building. It consists primarily of a single large space, with no distinction between nave and chancel, and yet it manages to combine a sense of the historic together with the excitement of the new. The layout of the building is unusual. Visitors enter at the East end, just to the South of the high altar, and follow a long ambulatory towards the back of the church. From here they turn back into the main body of the cathedral. By being expected to proceed along this route through the building they are following the historical tradition of a layout that required pilgrims to walk the longest way through a church to reach a shrine. The great space of the nave, 101 m (333 ft) long, provides a powerful contrast to the relatively narrow ambulatory. In fact once in the main body of the church the visitor is overwhelmed by the richly sculptured space within. This parallels the way in which the visitor to a mediaeval cathedral would have been astonished by the way that gothic walls, punctured by piers, colonnades, transepts and tracery, often seem indefinable and intriguing.

There are many other ways in which the designer, who was assisted by local architect Leo A. Daly, has managed to combine tradition with innovation. The walls of the cathedral are built from a pale honey-coloured concrete, but they are carefully detailed and have been cast in a sophisticated and controlled way. The result has the dignity of a massive stone building. Perhaps the most interesting element of the overall structure is the use of alabaster instead of glass for the windows, which allows a mellow, filtered light into the church. Alabaster was sometimes used in small quantities for openings in the ancient Romanesque churches that Moneo greatly admires.

Even the fittings combine the old and the new. The tapestries on the walls depict a triumphant Eastwards march of the saints of the Catholic Church, but they also act as sound absorbers. The elegant lamps that hang from the ceiling use triangular symbolism to represent the Trinity; at the centre of each lamp hangs a trumpet, associated with the traditional depiction of an angel but here, appropriately, also housing a loudspeaker.

The Cathedral of Our Lady of the Angels, Los Angeles, was designed by Rafael Moneo and completed in 2002. Its windows are glazed with alabaster panels.

The last great monument of the master of Modernism

St Pierre, Firminy-Vert, Loire, France

HERE IS A CHURCH that at first sight seems to be a different type of building from all the others, and yet demonstrates that the traditional aims and aspirations of church builders everywhere in the world continued to be revitalized up to the end of the twentieth century.

The great Swiss architect Le Corbusier, considered by many to be the most inspiring architect of his era, died aged 78 in 1965. Just before his death he had drawn up an urban scheme for the industrial town of Firminy to the south-west of Lyon. It was not until 1973 that the church of St Pierre, the centrepiece of his plan, began to go up. Work was abandoned halfway; following a later threat of demolition, however, building was eventually restarted under the direction of Le Corbusier's collabora-tor José Oubrerie and completed in December 2006. Ironically, the building although recognized as a national monument is not actually a consecrated, functioning church: had it been one, it would have been ineligible to receive the state aid it needed for its completion. The building's main practical use at present is as an art gallery, which occupies the space on the lower floors intended by the architect as parish rooms and the priest's accommodation.

St Pierre is a massive inhabitable concrete sculpture shaped like an inverted and sliced funnel, and derives its effect from the intense aesthetic experience it provokes. The funnel has few openings: a scattering of tiny holes in its shell repro-duce the constellation of Orion, and three deep geometrical apertures on the roof and walls, painted in primary colours, project bold shafts of light. A ring of smaller windows follows the path of a massive gutter around the exterior. Nearly all the fittings, including the pulpit, bishop's throne and tabernacle, are cast in concrete. The atmosphere is primitive yet paradoxically sophisticated and evocative – the aim of church builders throughout the centuries.

Designing churches for the future

NEW CHURCHES will continue to be an exciting combination of innovatory forms with some of the most familiar ideas in European culture. It always seems possible to look back to the concepts on which Christianity is based – renewal, redemption, hope – and find new ways of expressing them. Every generation will continue to decide what is important in life and in their beliefs, and look to the church to demonstrate it in its symbolic art and architecture.

Some churches have succeeded in providing their congregation with a great richness of experience in spite of their small size and limited budget. One of the most successful recent examples can be found at a church in Mortensrud, just outside Oslo, that was designed by the Norwegian architects Jensen & Skodvin, and opened in 2002.

The church is built on a rocky outcrop that is closely planted with pine trees. The structure of the church is reminiscent of agricultural building: it is a simple steel frame, with panels infilled at their upper level with large pieces of slate freely arranged as they might be in drystone walling and protected by panes of glass. Inside, the rock breaks through the floor towards the East and West ends, which has the effect of stressing the close relationship between the basic elements and demands of Christian life with the natural laws of the environment. Some have also seen a connection between the farm-like design of the building and the stable where Jesus was born in Bethlehem. The bright Nordic light filters in very subtly through the gaps between the pieces of slate, and so the church has the changing, mystical quality that one might expect but without the use of expensive materials. At the lower level the view from inside is of the trees. The campanile outside perhaps resembles a forest lookout more than it does the traditional bell tower.

The fittings inside the church were designed by Terje Hope, and they are mostly restrained and minimal. The reredos by Gunnar Torvlund, however, is a sparkling composition in gold and blue that combines traditional symbols such as the eye and the fish with new ones drawn from the contemporary life of the Church. The contrast between this and the subdued palette of the rest of the building is very powerful.

NEXT PAGE
Mortensrud church, outside Oslo. This powerful yet simple building was one of the first truly memorable parish churches to be completed in the twenty-first century.

As with any successful church building, the visitor to Mortensrud will never quite forget the experience. Perhaps there is no other aspect of architectural history anywhere in the world that is quite as rewarding as the discovery of an unfamiliar church.

Further reading

THE MOST useful books for anyone interested in knowing more about particular churches are the county guides in the *Buildings of England* series. Founded and originally edited by Nikolaus Pevsner, each town and village entry starts with a detailed description of local churches. They are now published by Yale University Press and are easily available.

Another important reference book is Stephen Friar's *A Companion to the English Parish Church* (Sutton, 2003). This provides a great deal of accessible information about the history, practices and architecture of the Church of England. The definitive academic work on these subjects, especially the history of theological arguments, is the *Oxford Dictionary of the Christian Church*, edited by F.L. Cross and E.A. Livingstone (OUP, 2005), and it should be available in libraries.

A further basic work of reference, and one which is indispensable to anyone with a serious interest in architecture, is the *Oxford Dictionary of Architecture and Landscape Architecture*, by James Stevens Curl (OUP, 2006).

Two useful and well-known guides can sometimes be found second-hand. These are the *Collins Guide to Parish Churches of England and Wales: including the Isle of Man*, edited by John Betjeman (Collins, last published 1968); and the *Faber Guide to Victorian Churches*, edited by Peter Howell and Ian Sutton (Faber, 1989).

Other books are a matter of personal preference. *England's Thousand Best Churches* by Simon Jenkins is a favourite for many (Penguin, 2000). A thorough guide with useful sections on details of church furnishings and traditions is *Harris's Guide to Churches and Cathedrals*, by Brian Harris (Ebury Press, 2006).

Here are some other recommended books with further detailed information on subjects referred to:

Cathedrals and mediaeval architecture:

Clifton-Taylor, Alec, *The Cathedrals of England* (Thames & Hudson, 1986)

Coldstream, Nicola, *Medieval Architecture* (OUP, 2002)

Stalley, Roger, *Early Medieval Architecture* (OUP, 1999)

Vicarage and rectory architecture:

Brittain-Catlin, Timothy, *The English Parsonage in the Early Nineteenth Century* (Spire, 2008)

The Reformation:

Duffy, Eamon, *The Stripping of the Altars* (Yale, 1992)

English classical church architecture:

Summerson, John, *Architecture in Britain, 1530 to 1830* (Yale, 1993)

English Victorian churches:

Curl, James Stevens, *Piety Proclaimed* (Historical Publications, 2002)

Roman Catholic churches in England and Wales:

Martin, Christopher, *A Glimpse of Heaven* (English Heritage, 2006)

Church furnishings and imagery:

Atterbury, Paul & Wainwright, Clive (eds), *Pugin: a Gothic Passion* (Yale/V&A, 1994)

Harrison, Martin, *Victorian Stained Glass* (Barrie & Jenkins, 1980)

Taylor, Richard, *How to Read a Church* (Rider, 2004)

Historical church architecture internationally:

Anker, Leif & Havran, Jiri, *The Norwegian Stave Churches* (ARFO, Oslo, 2005)

Frankl, Paul, *Gothic Architecture* (Yale, 2002)

Krautheimer, Richard, *Early Christian and Byzantine Architecture* (Yale, 1986)

Nussbaum, Norbert, *German Gothic Church Architecture* (Yale, 2000)

Opačić, Zoë, *Diamond Vaults* (Architectural Association, 2005)

Churches in Los Angeles:

Berger, Roger & Willis, Alfred, *Sacred Spaces: Historic Houses of Worship in the City of Angels* (Princeton Architectural Press/Balcony Press, 2004)

Twentieth-century and contemporary church architecture:

Heathcote, Edwin & Moffatt, Laura, *Contemporary Church Architecture* (John Wiley & Sons, 2007)

Richardson, Phyllis, *New Sacred Architecture* (Laurence King, 2004)

Stock, Wolfgang Jean, *European Church Architecture 1900–1950* (Prestel, 2006)

Stock, Wolfgang Jean, *European Church Architecture 1950–2000* (Prestel, 2003)

Glossary

These are the most common terms you are likely to encounter or need on a visit to a parish church.

Achievement
Full heraldic coat of arms with a helmet or coronet and sometimes supporters

Advent
Church season leading up to Christmas

Advowson
Patron's right to present a person to a living

Aisles
A continuous space through a building, usually referring to the areas either side of a church nave

Almshouse
Charitable home for the poor

Altar
Ancient and pre-Reformation name for what would now be described as a permanent communion table

Altarpiece
Decorative panel in a reredos

Ambulatory
Walkway in a large church

Amenity group/society
A publicly recognized organization that gives opinions on historic buildings

Anglican
Of the Church of England or a Church allied to it

Anglo-Catholic
Anglican who emphasizes mediaeval-type ritual

Apostle
One of Jesus' original supporters

Apse
Rounded or polygonal recess

Art Nouveau
Late nineteenth/early twentieth century non-historical style characterized by organic ornament

Assistant curate
Assistant to a priest

Aumbry
Recess

Aureole
Bright background to a figure

Authorised Version
Version of the Bible approved by King James I in 1611

Baldachino
Fixed canopy, properly with curtains

Banns
Announcement of a forthcoming marriage

Baptism
Ceremony of admission to the Church

Barrel vault
Semicircular vault

Basilica
Large room lit by clerestory windows above lean-to aisles the length of the long sides

Bell-cote
Roof-mounted structure for bells

Benefice
Holding of an ecclesiastical position, usually the incumbency of a parish

Blessed sacrament
Bread and wine consecrated during the eucharist

Blind arcade
An arcade along a wall but without openings

Book of Common Prayer
The approved form of worship in an Anglican church, usually referring to the 1662 edition

Boss
Structural projection, usually decorated, at the junction of vault ribs

Buttress
A masonry projection added to a wall to stiffen it

Calme/came
Lead strip connecting pieces of stained glass

Capital
Decorative head of column

Cartoon
Drawing used as an intermediate stage when creating artwork

Celebrant
Person conducting service of eucharist

Cemetery
Graveyard not connected with church

Chancel
Architecturally distinct part of church to the East of the nave containing the sanctuary

Chancel arch
Arch separating nave from chancel

Chancellor
Chief legal adviser to diocese

Chancel screen
Screen dividing chancel from nave

Change-ringing
Combinations of ringing bells

Chantry
Endowed or previously endowed private chapel with tomb

Chapter
The members of a monastic or religious order

Chapter house
Meeting room for cathedral staff

Choir
A group of parish or cathedral singers but also, in a larger church, the area where they sit.

Christmas
Celebration of Jesus' birth

Churchwarden
An elected or co-opted member of a parochial church council, chosen to manage local parish and church matters

Ciborium
In architecture, a domed fixed canopy

Clapham Sect
Late eighteenth-century evangelical leaders

Clerestory
Upper part of wall, usually of nave, with windows admitting daylight

Colonette
Small column, often in a cluster

Commissioners' church
Nineteenth-century church built with the help of state money following an 1818 act of parliament and successive legislation

Common Worship
Service book authorized by the Church of
England in 2000

Communion rail
Low rail in front of altar

Communion table
Table for celebrating the eucharist

Confessional
Booth where a priest hears private confession
in Roman Catholic churches

Confirmation
Ceremony where person renews baptismal
vows, usually as a young teenager

Consistory court
Senior legal authority of a diocese

Credence table
Shelf or table in chancel for the sacraments

Crocket
A carved floral ornament often shaped like a
leaf or bud and usually found along the edges
of gothic stone or timberwork

Crossing
The area in a cathedral or large church where
the transepts intersect the nave

Crypt
The basement storey of a church

Curate
Properly, any clergyman – but in practice an
assistant priest

Curvilinear tracery
Elaborate late Decorated tracery featuring
many flowing lines

DAC
Diocesan advisory committee

Daggers
Decorative tracery pattern like a teardrop with
two pointed ends

Decorated
Style of gothic architecture prevalent from late
thirteenth to mid-fourteenth centuries,
characterized by traceried windows and
densely carved ornament

Defrocked
Deprived of clerical status

Diamond vault
Ornamental multi-faceted vault without ribs

Diocese
The area under the authority of a bishop

Diocesan advisory committee
Diocesan group that advises on alterations or
additions to church buildings

Dissenters
English Christians not members of the Church
of England

Early English
First period of the English gothic style,
prevalent from late twelfth to late thirteenth
century, characterized by narrow pointed
windows without tracery

Easter
Celebration of Jesus' resurrection from the
dead

Eastern Church
General name for the East European and
Russian Orthodox Churches, now united as
the Eastern Orthodox Church

Easter sepulchre
Symbolic tomb used in pre-Reformation
worship

Ecclesiastical
Of the Church

Encaustic tile
Tile with embedded decorative colour

Entablature
In classical architecture, the horizontal line of
masonry directly above a row of columns

Epiphany
Celebration on 6th January of Jesus'
presentation to the three kings

Episcopal/ian
Church system with bishops, usually referring
to an Anglican Church outside England

Eucharist

Celebration of Jesus' last supper where wine and bread become sacraments

Evangelical

In Anglican context, movement that emphasizes preaching over ritual

Evangelist

Matthew, Mark, Luke or John

Evensong

Evening service of the Church of England

Faculty

Ecclesiastical permission, for example to alter a church

Fan vault

Decorative vault with downward projections like cones or half-cones

Finials

Decorative upward projection

Flamboyant tracery/style

Tracery with flame-like curvy lines, usually French

Flying buttresses

Masonry column placed away from a wall but part of a structural system intended to stiffen it

Font

Receptacle for water used in baptism ceremony

Frontal

Coloured, often embroidered panel fixed to front of communion table

Gargoyle

Decorative masonry figure, usually a waterspout

Geometrical tracery

Tracery with simple geometrical patterns

Glebe

Church land in a parish, originally to support the parson

Gospels

The first four books of the New Testament

Groin vault

Simple masonry vault, with junctions without ribs

Grozing iron

Tool used for fine cutting of stained glass prior to assembly

Hall church

Church where aisles are as tall as the nave

Hammerbeam roof

Type of roof supported on long inward-projecting brackets

Hatchment

Heraldic panel used for funeral processions

Holy communion

A name for the eucharist

Hunky punk

Type of carved squatting figure, characteristic of Somerset in Southwest England

Iconography

System of presenting religious symbolism in art

Impost mouldings

Decorative top of a gothic pier

Incumbent

Vicar or rector with a benefice

Intersecting tracery

Simple window tracery where curving mullions intersect

Jesse tree

Representation of family tree from Jesse to Jesus

Labarum

Greek monogram for Jesus' name resembling superimposed X and P

Lady chapel

Chapel dedicated to Mary, mother of Jesus

Lancet
Narrow window with a pointed top, typical of
Early English architecture
Lay rector
Person without ecclesiastical qualification
but with particular rights and responsibilities
in a church
Lectern
Book rest used when reading aloud from a
bible during a service
Lent
Church season of penance preceding
Easter
Lesene
Shallow buttress-like projection on
Romanesque buildings
Lierne
Subsidary rib on vault
Liturgical
As required by the conventions of church
services
Living
Another word for a benefice – the holding
of an ecclesiastical position, usually the
incumbency of a parish
Lychgate
Roofed gate into churchyard from street.

Mandorla
Pointed oval shape
Manorial church
Church closely linked to a manor house
Martyrium
Structure built over a tomb
Mass
Roman Catholic term for the eucharist
Matins
Morning service of the Church of England
Matriarch
The biblical Sarah, Rebecca, Rachel
and Leah – the wives of the patriarchs

Misericords
Carved ledge attached to folding stall seat
Mouchettes
Teardrop-shaped tracery pattern

Nave
Main body of a church where
the congregation sit, to the West of
a chancel
Niche
A recess
Nonconformists
English Christians not members of the
Church of England

Oxford Movement
Victorian religious movement that aimed to
emulate the pre-Reformation English Church

Parable
Metaphorical story told by Jesus in the Gospels
Parclose screen
A screen separating a chapel from others or
from the chancel
Parish
The smallest unit of local government
and of church authority
Parish chest
Repository for parish records
Parochial church council
The church's managing committee, including
the incumbent and various elected and co-
opted members
Parson
An old-fashioned word for an incumbent
Passion
The events of the final week of Jesus' life
Pastoral measure
Legally binding Church instruction relating to
the parish management
Patriarch
The biblical Abraham, Isaac and Jacob

PCC
Parochial church council

Pendentives
Curved triangular pieces of masonry connecting a dome to an orthogonal base

Pentecost
A celebration of the Holy Spirit 50 days after Easter Sunday

Perpendicular
Late style of English gothic architecture characterized by broad windows and reduced wall space

Perpetual curate
Type of incumbent, neither vicar nor rector, merged with vicars in 1868

Pew
Formerly private church seating in the form of an enclosed box

Pier
The usual word for a column when describing Romanesque or gothic architecture

Piscina
Stone basin for rinsing vessels used at the eucharist

Plate
The metal dishes and chalice used at the eucharist

Plate tracery
Flat window tracery

Poor relief
Historic type of parish financial support for the poor

Predella
Platform for the communion table at the East end of a church, or a ledge above or on an altar to support an altarpiece

Presbytery
An area in a church chancel or cathedral East of the choir and including the sanctuary

Priest
General term for a holder of any ecclesiastical office

Prismatory
A group of sedilia

Prophet
Old Testament figure who was inspired to teach the word of God and spread his messages

Protestant
The general term for a Western Christian, or Christian Church, independent of the Roman Catholic Church and following Lutheran principles

Pulpit
A raised platform for preaching

Pulpitum
A substantial stone screen between nave and choir in a large church

Quadripartite vault
Vault whose bays are divided by ribs into four parts

Rayonnant
French tracery style characterized by radiating tracery

Rector
Originally an incumbent who received the great tithes; now simply a title for an incumbent or the leader of a team ministry

Reformation
The historical process by which the English Church first became independent of papal control and subsequently Protestant

Reordering
The permanent moving of important church furnishings and fittings, usually for liturgical reasons

Reredos
Decorated panel behind the communion table

Responds
A partial pier fixed against the wall of an arcade rising to the vault

Restoration
The accession of Charles II to the throne of England after the Cromwellian Interregnum

Retable
Frame or setting for a reredos

Reticulated tracery
Net-like tracery

Retrochoir
Area in large church or cathedral East of the high altar

Rib
Raised ceiling moulding, usually structural

Roman Catholic
Member of the Christian Church under the authority of the pope

Romanesque
Pre-gothic style of architecture characterized by heavy masonry, small windows and semi-circular arches

Rood
Depiction of Jesus' crucifixion, flanked by Mary and St John the Evangelist

Rood beam
A beam supporting a rood

Rood loft
Gallery above a rood screen

Rood screen
Chancel screen below a rood

Rood stair
Stair to reach a rood loft

Royal Peculiar
Large church under the authority of the Crown rather than of a bishop

Sacristy
Church room for storing church plate

Saint
A person recognized by the Church for their martyrdom or the ability to work miracles in the name of Jesus

Sanctuary
Area immediately around the communion table, usually raised

Sedilia
Built-in seats on the South side of the sanctuary. Singular: sedile.

Sermon
Address by a preacher to the congregation

Sexpartite vault
Vault whose bays are divided by ribs into six parts

Sheela-na-gig
Type of indecent carving of a woman

Shell vault
Type of fan vault where ribs and webs are structurally indistinguishable

Shrine
Place dedicated to the veneration of a deceased person, sometimes formerly (or today in some Roman Catholic churches) containing relics of their body

Sounding board
Acoustic panel above a pulpit

Spandrel
Piece of wall in the approximately triangular area between two arches

Spire
Pointed construction rising from a church tower

Squarson
Historical term for parson who was a member of the gentry

Squint
Spy hole allowing visual connection between a chapel and a high altar

Stalls
Seats facing North and South in choir or presbytery

Stations of the cross
Scenes from Jesus' last days

Stave church
Ancient Norwegian timber church

Steeple
Church tower and spire together

Stiff leaf
Type of stylized foliage carving

Stoup
Small basin for holy water

Synod

A formal Church assembly. The General Synod is the parliament of the Church of England

Tabernacle

Ornamental box or niche

Team ministry

Incumbents that work together across a group of parishes

Ten commandments

The ten basic laws of Judaism and Christianity given by God to Moses on Mount Sinai

Terrier

Ecclesiastical inventory

Tester

Acoustic panel above a pulpit

Thirty-nine articles

The fundamental doctrinal beliefs of the Church of England

Tie-beam roof

A roof structure held together by horizontal beams along its base

Tierceron rib

Rib that runs from the top of the wall to a position along the ridge

Tithe

Historic tax on agricultural produce that supported the church and its parson

Tracery

Ornamental stone carving, usually on windows

Transept

A part of a cathedral or large church that projects from the North and South sides of the nave or chancel

Tribune

Gallery, sometimes in the form of a triforium

Triforium

Upper aisle above the main arcade in a large church

Trinity Sunday

The first Sunday after Pentecost

Trophy

Sculpture representing armour or weapons

Typology

Use of representational art to signify meaning

Vault

A length of an arched masonry ceiling

Vestments

Costume for use in church ceremonies

Vestry

Store room for church plate or vestments; originally the managing committee of a parish

Vicar

Originally an incumbent who received the little tithes; now simply a title for an incumbent

Voussoirs

Wedge-shaped stone in arch construction

Wagon roof

Ceiling with polygonal section

Web

The vault areas between the ribs

Western Church

The Roman Catholic and Protestant Churches in general

Workhouse

Before 1834, a place that dispensed parish assistance to the poor and unemployed; after 1834, a kind of prison for the same people

Worship space

Recent term for the area around a communion table that has been brought Westwards towards or into the nave as a result of reordering

Index

Acknowledgements

The author would like to thank the following for their help and advice: Catriona and Michael Blaker; Mark Bostridge; Daniel Brittain-Catlin; Herb Broderick; Desmond Day; Øystein Ekroll; Robert Floyd; Sallyann Ford; David Garrard; Max Gwiazda; David Hanson; Robert Hargrave; Peter Howell; Charles Lutyens; Canon David Meara; Rory O'Donnell; Zoë Opačić; Jane Ridley; Andrew Rudd; Andrew Saint; John Scott; Charles Smith; Jackie Withers; and Ellis Woodman.

Picture credits

All photographs by Amanda Stanley or public domain unless otherwise stated. Abbreviations: **b** bottom; **l** left; **r** right; **t** top. **10, 13** Library of Congress; **15** © R Neil Marshman/Creative Commons Licence; **16** courtesy of Ordnance Survey; **19, 21** Library of Congress; **24** © The British Library/Heritage image partnership; **28l, r** © Getty Images; **30** courtesy of The President and Fellows of Magdalen College, Oxford/© John Gibbons; **31** Library of Congress; **33** courtesy of Hampshire Record Office; **34** © The Nailsea Tithe Barn Trust; **35t** © Simon Chalton; **35b** © Neil Setchtfield/Alamy; **36** ©T Chalcraft/Creative Commons Licence; **37** © All rights reserved.The British Library Board; **38** © Bridgeman; **41** © Alf/GNU Free Documentation Licence; **43** © Archie Miles/Alamy; **45** © Jason Bye/Alamy; **46** © Episcopal Life Media; **47** Library of Congress; **48** © TTaylor; **51** Creative Commons Licence; **53** © Basement Press; **54** © Necrothesp/GNU Free Documentation Licence; **55** © Nils Jorgensen/Rex Features; **59** © Ingo Rickmann/Creative Commons Licence; **61** © Charlie Newham/Alamy; **63** © Adam Woolfitt/Corbis; **65** © Heritage image partnership; **66** © photos.com; **69** © Yann Arthus-Bertrand/Corbis; **71** © Necrothesp/GNU Free Documentation Licence; **73** © Guy Edwardes photography/Alamy; **75t** © TomAlt/Creative Commons Licence; **75b** © Robert Harding Picture LIbrary Ltd/Alamy; **76** © David Gee/Alamy; **77l** © London Aerial Photo Library/Corbis; **77r** © Julie Woodhouse/Alamy; **78l** © Jan van der Crabben/Creative Commons Licence; **78r** © Peter Garbet/Alamy; **80** © photos.com; **81** © Ben Ramos/Alamy; **82** © Angelo Hornak/Corbis; **83** © Gordon Nicholson/Heritage image partnership; **84** © Andrew Paterson/Alamy; **85** © Keith Jones/Heritage image partnership; **86** Library of Congress; **91** © J.K. Hansom; **92** © Basement Press; **97** © J Bailey/Heritage image partnership; **98** © Greenshoots Communications/Alamy; **103** © Chris Bland - Eye Ubiquitous/Corbis; **110** © Rupert Horrox/Corbis; **116** © photos.com; **120** © John Salmon; **121** © Hulton-Deutsch Collection/Corbis; **122** © Getty Images; **123** © Basement Press; **127** © Heritage image partnership; **129** © St Paul's Hammersmith; **130** © Imagebroker/ Alamy; **134** © Manor Photography/Alamy; **137** © Peter Stubbs, Edinburgh, at www.edinphoto.org.uk; **138** © Heritage image partnership; **139** © Marc Hill/Alamy; **142** © Iona Robertson; **143** © David Poole/Alamy; **144** © Basement Press; **145** © Dorothy Burrows/Heritage image partnership; **149** © Michael Jenner/Alamy; **150** © Arcaid/Corbis; **152** © Museum of London/Heritage image partnership; **154** © Heritage image partnership; **161** © City of London Libraries and Guildhall Art Gallery/Heritage image partnership; **162** © John Salmon; **165** © Basement Press; **167** © Martin Charles; **169** © Basement Press; **174** © photos.com; **176** © Laurence Goldman/Heritage image partnership; **182, 187** © Derek Anson/Heritage image partnership; **191** © Basement Press; **193, 199** © Martin Charles; **200** © Ken Murrell/Heritage image partnership; **203** © Derek Anson/Heritage image partnership; **205** © Helen Harrison/Heritage image partnership; **206** Library of Congress; **207** © photos.com; **210** © Diana Kremer/GNU Free Documentation Licence; **211** © Wayne McLean/Creative Commons Licence; **212** © Babak Gholizadeh/Creative Commons Licence; **213** © Peter Thompson/Heritage image partnership; **215** © Martin Charles; **217** © Eitan Simanor/Alamy; **219** © photos.com; **220** © Bildarchiv Foto Marburg; **221** © Danita Delimont/Alamy; **222** © Sue Barr; **224** © Jan Sokol/Creative Commons Licence; **225** © Getty Images; **226** © Archivo Iconografico, S.A./Corbis; **227** © Noclip; **228** © Dezidor/Creative Commons Licence; **229** © Mallikarjun Katakol; **231** © RIBA Library Photographs Collection; **232** © Arcaid/Alamy; **235** © Art on File/Corbis; **237** ©Vincent Granger; **239** © Per Berntsen.